Copyright © 2020

All rights reserved. No part of this publication may be reproduced, stored in a retrieval system, or transmitted, in any form or by any means, electronic, mechanical, photocopying, recording, or otherwise, without the written prior permission of the publisher.

Introduction

Welcome!

Managing Social media sometimes seems like an uphill job.
So many different platforms. What to post on them all? When to post? And how to keep track of it all?

The thought behind this handbook is to encourage you to collect your thoughts in one spot.

>What are your writing ideas for the day?
>What are your thoughts for content on your blog?
>What tweets match your blog content?
>What tweets go with sales that you have ongoing?
>How to share this information on Facebook and so on?

This agenda has a variety of "thought collection pages," ideas from other authors & influencers and a lot of space to let your creativity shine!

DATE _____

MONDAY	TUESDAY	WEDNESDAY
☐	☐	☐
☐	☐	☐
☐	☐	☐
☐	☐	☐
☐	☐	☐

DATE _____

THURSDAY	FRIDAY	SATURDAY / SUNDAY
☐	☐	☐
☐	☐	☐
☐	☐	☐
☐	☐	☐
☐	☐	☐

DATE _____

Newsletter Thoughts

DATE _____

Book Promotion Plans

DATE _____

WRITING GOALS

SOCIAL MEDIA GOALS

BLOGGING GOALS

IMPORTANT ACTIVITIES FOR TODAY

- [ ]
- [ ]
- [ ]
- [ ]
- [ ]
- [ ]
- [ ]
- [ ]

> "Selling to people through social media is like going to a party, meeting somebody for the first time, and then saying, "Hey, do you want to buy this Tupperware?"
>
> ~Pat Flynn

DATE _____

SOCIAL MEDIA GOALS

[Facebook]

[Twitter]

[Instagram]

[Pinterest]

WRITING GOALS

BLOGGING GOALS

IMPORTANT ACTIVITIES FOR TODAY

- [ ]
- [ ]
- [ ]
- [ ]
- [ ]
- [ ]
- [ ]
- [ ]

> "Visual content is 40 times more likely to be shared on social media than any other type of content."

DATE _____

WRITING GOALS

BLOGGING GOALS

SOCIAL MEDIA GOALS

IMPORTANT ACTIVITIES FOR TODAY

- [ ]
- [ ]
- [ ]
- [ ]
- [ ]
- [ ]
- [ ]
- [ ]

> "Social media is not a media. The key is to listen, engage, and build relationships."
> ~David Alston

DATE _____

SOCIAL MEDIA GOALS

f

t

◉

P

WRITING GOALS

BLOGGING GOALS

IMPORTANT ACTIVITIES FOR TODAY

☐
☐
☐
☐
☐
☐
☐
☐

> "Engage rather than sell ... Work as a co-creator, not a marketer."
>
> ~ Tom H. C. Anderson

DATE _____

WRITING GOALS

BLOGGING GOALS

SOCIAL MEDIA GOALS

IMPORTANT ACTIVITIES FOR TODAY

"Activate your fans, don't just collect them like baseball cards."

~Jay Baer

DATE _____

SOCIAL MEDIA GOALS

[Facebook]

....
....
....
....

[Twitter]

....
....
....
....

[Instagram]

....
....
....
....

[Pinterest]

....
....
....
....

WRITING GOALS

....
....
....
....
....
....
....
....
....
....
....
....

BLOGGING GOALS

....
....
....
....
....
....
....
....

IMPORTANT ACTIVITIES FOR TODAY

- [ ]
- [ ]
- [ ]
- [ ]
- [ ]
- [ ]
- [ ]
- [ ]

"Focus on how to be social, not on how to do social."

~Jay Baer

DATE _____

WRITING GOALS

....
....
....
....
....
....
....
....
....
....

BLOGGING GOALS

....
....
....
....
....
....
....

SOCIAL MEDIA GOALS

f
....
....
....
....

Twitter
....
....
....
....

Instagram
....
....
....

Pinterest
....
....
....

"If you make customers unhappy in the physical world, they might each tell 6 friends. If you make customers unhappy on the Internet, they can each tell 6,000 friends."

~Jeff Bezos

IMPORTANT ACTIVITIES FOR TODAY

- [ ] ....
- [ ] ....
- [ ] ....
- [ ] ....
- [ ] ....
- [ ] ....
- [ ] ....
- [ ] ....

DATE _____

SOCIAL MEDIA GOALS

WRITING GOALS

BLOGGING GOALS

IMPORTANT ACTIVITIES FOR TODAY

- [ ]
- [ ]
- [ ]
- [ ]
- [ ]
- [ ]
- [ ]
- [ ]

> "Don't say anything online that you wouldn't want plastered on a billboard with your face on it."
>
> ~Erin Bury

DATE _____

WRITING GOALS

SOCIAL MEDIA GOALS

BLOGGING GOALS

IMPORTANT ACTIVITIES FOR TODAY

- [ ]
- [ ]
- [ ]
- [ ]
- [ ]
- [ ]
- [ ]
- [ ]

> "'Build it, and they will come' only works in the movies. Social Media is a 'build it, nurture it, engage them, and they may come and stay."
>
> ~Seth Godin

DATE _____

SOCIAL MEDIA GOALS

f
....
....
....
....

🐦
....
....
....
....

📷
....
....
....
....

P
....
....
....
....

WRITING GOALS

....
....
....
....
....
....
....
....
....
....

BLOGGING GOALS

....
....
....
....
....
....
....

IMPORTANT ACTIVITIES FOR TODAY

- [ ] ....
- [ ] ....
- [ ] ....
- [ ] ....
- [ ] ....
- [ ] ....
- [ ] ....
- [ ] ....

> "Conversations among the members of your marketplace happen whether you like it or not. Good marketing encourages the right sort of conversations.'"
>
> ~Seth Godin

DATE _____

WRITING GOALS

SOCIAL MEDIA GOALS

BLOGGING GOALS

IMPORTANT ACTIVITIES FOR TODAY

- [ ]
- [ ]
- [ ]
- [ ]
- [ ]
- [ ]
- [ ]
- [ ]

> "Social Media is about the people! Not about your business. Provide for the people and the people will provide for you."
>
> ~Matt Goulart

DATE _____

SOCIAL MEDIA GOALS

Facebook

Twitter

Instagram

Pinterest

WRITING GOALS

BLOGGING GOALS

IMPORTANT ACTIVITIES FOR TODAY

- [ ]
- [ ]
- [ ]
- [ ]
- [ ]
- [ ]
- [ ]
- [ ]

> "The value of being connected and transparent is so high that the roadbumps of privacy issues are much lower in actual experience than people's fears."
>
> ~Reid Hoffman

DATE _____

WRITING GOALS

SOCIAL MEDIA GOALS

[Facebook]

[Twitter]

[Instagram]

[Pinterest]

BLOGGING GOALS

> "Bring the best of your authentic self to every opportunity."
>
> ~Brian Jantsch

IMPORTANT ACTIVITIES FOR TODAY

- [ ]
- [ ]
- [ ]
- [ ]
- [ ]
- [ ]
- [ ]
- [ ]
- [ ]

DATE _____

SOCIAL MEDIA GOALS

f

WRITING GOALS

t

[Instagram]

BLOGGING GOALS

P

IMPORTANT ACTIVITIES FOR TODAY

- [ ]
- [ ]
- [ ]
- [ ]
- [ ]
- [ ]
- [ ]
- [ ]

> "Just be nice, take genuine interest in the people you meet, and keep in touch with people you like. This will create a group of people who are invested in helping you because they know you and appreciate you."
>
> ~Guy Kawasaki

DATE _____

WRITING GOALS

BLOGGING GOALS

SOCIAL MEDIA GOALS

IMPORTANT ACTIVITIES FOR TODAY

- [ ]
- [ ]
- [ ]
- [ ]
- [ ]
- [ ]
- [ ]
- [ ]

> "What happens in Vegas stays in Vegas; what happens on Twitter stays on Google forever!"
>
> ~Jure Klepic

DATE _____

SOCIAL MEDIA GOALS

WRITING GOALS

BLOGGING GOALS

IMPORTANT ACTIVITIES FOR TODAY

- [ ]
- [ ]
- [ ]
- [ ]
- [ ]
- [ ]
- [ ]
- [ ]

> "Most bloggers who rise above the clutter are quite often prolific – they work hard, not just writing content but networking, engaging in Social Media and more."
>
> ~Darren Rowse

DATE _____

WRITING GOALS

BLOGGING GOALS

SOCIAL MEDIA GOALS

[Facebook]

[Twitter]

[Instagram]

[Pinterest]

IMPORTANT ACTIVITIES FOR TODAY

- [ ]
- [ ]
- [ ]
- [ ]
- [ ]
- [ ]
- [ ]
- [ ]

> "There are no magic wands, no hidden tracks, and no secret handshakes that can bring you immediate success, but with time, energy and determination you can get there."
>
> ~Darren Rowse

DATE _____

SOCIAL MEDIA GOALS

f
....
....
....
....

🐦
....
....
....
....

📷
....
....
....
....

P
....
....
....
....

WRITING GOALS

....
....
....
....
....
....
....
....
....
....

BLOGGING GOALS

....
....
....
....
....
....
....

IMPORTANT ACTIVITIES FOR TODAY

☐ ....
☐ ....
☐ ....
☐ ....
☐ ....
☐ ....
☐ ....
☐ ....

> "The qualities that make Twitter seem insane and half-baked are what makes it so powerful."
>
> ~Jonathan Zittrain

DATE _____

WRITING GOALS

....
....
....
....
....
....
....
....
....
....

BLOGGING GOALS

....
....
....
....
....
....
....

SOCIAL MEDIA GOALS

f
....
....
....
....

t
....
....
....

IG
....
....

P
....
....
....

> "When you give everyone a voice and give people power, the system usually ends up in a really good place."
>
> ~Mark Zuckerberg

IMPORTANT ACTIVITIES FOR TODAY

- [ ] ....
- [ ] ....
- [ ] ....
- [ ] ....
- [ ] ....
- [ ] ....
- [ ] ....
- [ ] ....

DATE _____

SOCIAL MEDIA GOALS

f
....
....
....
....

🐦
....
....
....
....

📷
....
....
....
....

P
....
....
....
....

WRITING GOALS

....
....
....
....
....
....
....
....
....
....
....
....

BLOGGING GOALS

....
....
....
....
....
....
....

IMPORTANT ACTIVITIES FOR TODAY

☐ ....
☐ ....
☐ ....
☐ ....
☐ ....
☐ ....
☐ ....
☐ ....

> "Never underestimate the vital importance of finding early in life the work that for you is play. This turns possible underachievers into happy warriors."
>
> ~Jeff Bullas

DATE _____

WRITING GOALS

SOCIAL MEDIA GOALS

BLOGGING GOALS

IMPORTANT ACTIVITIES FOR TODAY

- [ ]
- [ ]
- [ ]
- [ ]
- [ ]
- [ ]
- [ ]
- [ ]

> "Social media is here. It's not going away; not a passing fad. Be where your customers are: in social media."
>
> ~Lori Ruff

DATE _____

SOCIAL MEDIA GOALS

WRITING GOALS

BLOGGING GOALS

IMPORTANT ACTIVITIES FOR TODAY

- [ ]
- [ ]
- [ ]
- [ ]
- [ ]
- [ ]
- [ ]
- [ ]

> "Most of us have experienced wow moments. We just haven't taken time to think deeply about them."
>
> ~Michael Hyatt

DATE _____

WRITING GOALS

SOCIAL MEDIA GOALS

BLOGGING GOALS

> "On engagement, we're already seeing that mobile users are more likely to be daily active users than desktop users. They're more likely to use Facebook six or seven days of the week."
>
> ~Mark Zuckerberg

IMPORTANT ACTIVITIES FOR TODAY

- [ ]
- [ ]
- [ ]
- [ ]
- [ ]
- [ ]
- [ ]
- [ ]

DATE _____

SOCIAL MEDIA GOALS

Facebook

Twitter

Instagram

Pinterest

WRITING GOALS

BLOGGING GOALS

IMPORTANT ACTIVITIES FOR TODAY

- [ ]
- [ ]
- [ ]
- [ ]
- [ ]
- [ ]
- [ ]
- [ ]

> "Facebook is not your friend. It is a surveillance engine."
>
> ~Richard Stallman

DATE _____

WRITING GOALS

SOCIAL MEDIA GOALS

BLOGGING GOALS

IMPORTANT ACTIVITIES FOR TODAY

- [ ]
- [ ]
- [ ]
- [ ]
- [ ]
- [ ]
- [ ]
- [ ]
- [ ]

> "Twitter is not a technology, it's a conversation – and it's happening with or without you."
>
> ~Charlene Li, author

DATE _____

SOCIAL MEDIA GOALS

f
....
....
....
....

🐦
....
....
....
....

📷
....
....
....
....

P
....
....
....
....

WRITING GOALS

....
....
....
....
....
....
....
....
....
....

BLOGGING GOALS

....
....
....
....
....
....
....

IMPORTANT ACTIVITIES FOR TODAY

- [ ] ....
- [ ] ....
- [ ] ....
- [ ] ....
- [ ] ....
- [ ] ....
- [ ] ....
- [ ] ....

> "When you've got 5 minutes to fill, Twitter is a great way to fill 35 minutes."
>
> ~Matt Cutts

DATE _____

WRITING GOALS

BLOGGING GOALS

SOCIAL MEDIA GOALS

IMPORTANT ACTIVITIES FOR TODAY

- [ ]
- [ ]
- [ ]
- [ ]
- [ ]
- [ ]
- [ ]
- [ ]

"Social media is not just a spoke on the wheel of marketing. It's becoming the way entire bicycles are built."

~Ryan Lilly, author

DATE _____

SOCIAL MEDIA GOALS

[Facebook]

[Twitter]

[Instagram]

[Pinterest]

WRITING GOALS

BLOGGING GOALS

IMPORTANT ACTIVITIES FOR TODAY

- [ ]
- [ ]
- [ ]
- [ ]
- [ ]
- [ ]
- [ ]
- [ ]

> "Social media will help you build up the loyalty of your current customers to the point that they will willingly, and for free, tell others about you."
>
> ~Bonnie Sainsbury

DATE _____

WRITING GOALS

SOCIAL MEDIA GOALS

BLOGGING GOALS

IMPORTANT ACTIVITIES FOR TODAY

- [ ]
- [ ]
- [ ]
- [ ]
- [ ]
- [ ]
- [ ]
- [ ]

> "The Art of Twitter is in the Re-tweet. You Must be Interesting."
>
> ~Peter Shankman

DATE _____

SOCIAL MEDIA GOALS

WRITING GOALS

BLOGGING GOALS

IMPORTANT ACTIVITIES FOR TODAY

- [ ]
- [ ]
- [ ]
- [ ]
- [ ]
- [ ]
- [ ]
- [ ]

> "It's important to think of every customer as an on-line celebrity with followers, friends, & above all, influence."
>
> ~Dave Kerpen

DATE _____

MONDAY	TUESDAY	WEDNESDAY
☐	☐	☐
☐	☐	☐
☐	☐	☐
☐	☐	☐
☐	☐	☐

DATE _____

THURSDAY	FRIDAY	SATURDAY / SUNDAY
☐	☐	☐
☐	☐	☐
☐	☐	☐
☐	☐	☐
☐	☐	☐

DATE _____

Newsletter Thoughts

DATE _____

Book Promotion Plans

DATE _____

WRITING GOALS

SOCIAL MEDIA GOALS

BLOGGING GOALS

IMPORTANT ACTIVITIES FOR TODAY

- [ ]
- [ ]
- [ ]
- [ ]
- [ ]
- [ ]
- [ ]
- [ ]

> "As with any relationship, the market favors those who give more value than they ask for."
>
> ~Leslie Bradshaw

DATE _____

SOCIAL MEDIA GOALS

[Facebook]

[Twitter]

[Instagram]

[Pinterest]

WRITING GOALS

BLOGGING GOALS

IMPORTANT ACTIVITIES FOR TODAY

- [ ]
- [ ]
- [ ]
- [ ]
- [ ]
- [ ]
- [ ]
- [ ]

> "The ultimate content strategy is listening."
> – Marcus Sheridan

DATE _____

WRITING GOALS

BLOGGING GOALS

SOCIAL MEDIA GOALS

IMPORTANT ACTIVITIES FOR TODAY

- [ ]
- [ ]
- [ ]
- [ ]
- [ ]
- [ ]
- [ ]
- [ ]

> "You're never as smart as you think you are when you are winning and never as dumb as you feel when you are losing."
>
> ~Michael Hyatt

DATE _____

SOCIAL MEDIA GOALS

f

🐦

📷

P

WRITING GOALS

BLOGGING GOALS

IMPORTANT ACTIVITIES FOR TODAY

- [ ]
- [ ]
- [ ]
- [ ]
- [ ]
- [ ]
- [ ]
- [ ]

> "You can't take care of anyone else unless you first take care of yourself."
>
> ~Michael Hyatt

DATE _____

WRITING GOALS

BLOGGING GOALS

SOCIAL MEDIA GOALS

IMPORTANT ACTIVITIES FOR TODAY

- [ ]
- [ ]
- [ ]
- [ ]
- [ ]
- [ ]
- [ ]
- [ ]

> "Courage is the willingness to act in spite of fear."
> ~Michael Hyatt

DATE _____

SOCIAL MEDIA GOALS

WRITING GOALS

BLOGGING GOALS

IMPORTANT ACTIVITIES FOR TODAY

- [ ]
- [ ]
- [ ]
- [ ]
- [ ]
- [ ]
- [ ]
- [ ]

> "Make sure your worst enemy doesn't live between your two ears."
>
> ~Laird Hamilton

DATE _____

WRITING GOALS

BLOGGING GOALS

SOCIAL MEDIA GOALS

IMPORTANT ACTIVITIES FOR TODAY

- [ ]
- [ ]
- [ ]
- [ ]
- [ ]
- [ ]
- [ ]
- [ ]

> "The greatest danger for most of us is not that we aim too high and we miss it, but we aim too low and reach it."
>
> ~ Michelangelo

DATE _____

SOCIAL MEDIA GOALS

f

t

📷

P

WRITING GOALS

BLOGGING GOALS

IMPORTANT ACTIVITIES FOR TODAY

- [ ]
- [ ]
- [ ]
- [ ]
- [ ]
- [ ]
- [ ]
- [ ]

> "You don't need more opportunity. You need to learn to execute on the opportunities you already have."
>
> ~Michael Hyatt

DATE _____

WRITING GOALS

....
....
....
....
....
....
....
....
....
....
....

BLOGGING GOALS

....
....
....
....
....
....
....

SOCIAL MEDIA GOALS

f
....
....
....
....

t
....
....
....
....

ig
....
....
....
....

p
....
....
....
....

> "You can't start the next chapter of your life if you keep re-reading the last one."
>
> ~Anonymous

IMPORTANT ACTIVITIES FOR TODAY

- [ ] ....
- [ ] ....
- [ ] ....
- [ ] ....
- [ ] ....
- [ ] ....
- [ ] ....
- [ ] ....

DATE _____

SOCIAL MEDIA GOALS

[Facebook]

[Twitter]

[Instagram]

[Pinterest]

WRITING GOALS

BLOGGING GOALS

IMPORTANT ACTIVITIES FOR TODAY

- [ ]
- [ ]
- [ ]
- [ ]
- [ ]
- [ ]
- [ ]
- [ ]

> "In a crowded marketplace, fitting in a failure. In a busy marketplace, not standing out is the same as being invisible."
>
> ~Seth Godin

DATE _____

WRITING GOALS

BLOGGING GOALS

SOCIAL MEDIA GOALS

IMPORTANT ACTIVITIES FOR TODAY

- [ ]
- [ ]
- [ ]
- [ ]
- [ ]
- [ ]
- [ ]
- [ ]

> "I learned that a long walk and calm conversation are an incredible combination if you want to build a bridge."
>
> ~Seth Godin

DATE _____

SOCIAL MEDIA GOALS

WRITING GOALS

BLOGGING GOALS

IMPORTANT ACTIVITIES FOR TODAY

- [ ]
- [ ]
- [ ]
- [ ]
- [ ]
- [ ]
- [ ]
- [ ]

> "Marketing is a contest for people's attention."
>
> ~Seth Godin

DATE _____

WRITING GOALS

SOCIAL MEDIA GOALS

f

t

IG

BLOGGING GOALS

P

> "I think the most productive thing to do during times of change is to be your best self, not the best version of someone else."
>
> ~Seth Godin

IMPORTANT ACTIVITIES FOR TODAY

- [ ]
- [ ]
- [ ]
- [ ]
- [ ]
- [ ]
- [ ]
- [ ]

DATE _____

SOCIAL MEDIA GOALS

WRITING GOALS

BLOGGING GOALS

IMPORTANT ACTIVITIES FOR TODAY

- [ ]
- [ ]
- [ ]
- [ ]
- [ ]
- [ ]
- [ ]
- [ ]

> "Do you know what people want more than anything? They want to be missed. They want to be missed the day they don't show up. They want to be missed when they're gone."
>
> ~Seth Godin

DATE _____

WRITING GOALS

SOCIAL MEDIA GOALS

BLOGGING GOALS

IMPORTANT ACTIVITIES FOR TODAY

- [ ]
- [ ]
- [ ]
- [ ]
- [ ]
- [ ]
- [ ]
- [ ]

> "One reason I encourage people to blog is that the act of doing it stretches your available vocabulary and hones a new voice."
>
> ~Seth Godin

DATE _____

SOCIAL MEDIA GOALS

f
....
....
....
....

t
....
....
....
....

ig
....
....
....
....

p
....
....
....

WRITING GOALS

....
....
....
....
....
....
....
....
....
....
....

BLOGGING GOALS

....
....
....
....
....
....
....
....

IMPORTANT ACTIVITIES FOR TODAY

- [ ] ....
- [ ] ....
- [ ] ....
- [ ] ....
- [ ] ....
- [ ] ....
- [ ] ....
- [ ] ....

> "Permission marketing turns strangers into friends and friends into loyal customers. It's not just about entertainment – it's about education. Permission marketing is curriculum marketing."
>
> ~Seth Godin

DATE _____

WRITING GOALS

SOCIAL MEDIA GOALS

BLOGGING GOALS

IMPORTANT ACTIVITIES FOR TODAY

- [ ]
- [ ]
- [ ]
- [ ]
- [ ]
- [ ]
- [ ]
- [ ]

> "I made a decision to write for my readers, not to try to find more readers for my writing."
>
> ~Seth Godin

DATE _____

SOCIAL MEDIA GOALS

f
....
....
....
....

t
....
....
....
....

i
....
....
....
....

p
....
....
....
....

WRITING GOALS

....
....
....
....
....
....
....
....
....
....

BLOGGING GOALS

....
....
....
....
....
....
....

IMPORTANT ACTIVITIES FOR TODAY

- [ ] ....
- [ ] ....
- [ ] ....
- [ ] ....
- [ ] ....
- [ ] ....
- [ ] ....
- [ ] ....

"Stop getting distracted by things that have nothing to do with your dreams."

DATE _____

WRITING GOALS

SOCIAL MEDIA GOALS

BLOGGING GOALS

> "Stop telling yourself you don't know what to do. Yes, you do. Listen to your intuition and trust yourself."
>
> ~Katherine Sullivan

IMPORTANT ACTIVITIES FOR TODAY

- [ ]
- [ ]
- [ ]
- [ ]
- [ ]
- [ ]
- [ ]
- [ ]

DATE _____

SOCIAL MEDIA GOALS

[Facebook]

[Twitter]

[Instagram]

[Pinterest]

WRITING GOALS

BLOGGING GOALS

IMPORTANT ACTIVITIES FOR TODAY

- [ ]
- [ ]
- [ ]
- [ ]
- [ ]
- [ ]
- [ ]
- [ ]

> "Don't ask people for directions when they've never been where you are going."
>
> ~Katherine Sullivan

DATE _____

WRITING GOALS

SOCIAL MEDIA GOALS

Facebook

Twitter

Instagram

Pinterest

BLOGGING GOALS

> "Don't use social media to impress people; use it to impact people."
> ~Dave Willis

IMPORTANT ACTIVITIES FOR TODAY

- [ ]
- [ ]
- [ ]
- [ ]
- [ ]
- [ ]
- [ ]
- [ ]

DATE _____

SOCIAL MEDIA GOALS

f
....
....
....
....

t
....
....
....
....

ig
....
....
....
....

p
....
....
....
....

WRITING GOALS

....
....
....
....
....
....
....
....
....

BLOGGING GOALS

....
....
....
....
....
....
....

IMPORTANT ACTIVITIES FOR TODAY

- [ ] ....
- [ ] ....
- [ ] ....
- [ ] ....
- [ ] ....
- [ ] ....
- [ ] ....
- [ ] ....

"Be Authentic."

DATE _____

WRITING GOALS

SOCIAL MEDIA GOALS

f

t

ig

p

BLOGGING GOALS

"A goal should scare you a little, & excite you A LOT."

~Joe Vitale

IMPORTANT ACTIVITIES FOR TODAY

- [ ]
- [ ]
- [ ]
- [ ]
- [ ]
- [ ]
- [ ]
- [ ]

DATE _____

SOCIAL MEDIA GOALS

f

🐦

📷

P

WRITING GOALS

BLOGGING GOALS

IMPORTANT ACTIVITIES FOR TODAY

- ☐
- ☐
- ☐
- ☐
- ☐
- ☐
- ☐
- ☐

> "Surround yourself with those on the same mission as you."

DATE _____

WRITING GOALS

SOCIAL MEDIA GOALS

BLOGGING GOALS

IMPORTANT ACTIVITIES FOR TODAY

- [ ]
- [ ]
- [ ]
- [ ]
- [ ]
- [ ]
- [ ]
- [ ]

"It's your road, and yours alone. Others may walk it with you, but no one can walk it for you."

~ Rumi

DATE _____

SOCIAL MEDIA GOALS

WRITING GOALS

BLOGGING GOALS

IMPORTANT ACTIVITIES FOR TODAY

- [ ]
- [ ]
- [ ]
- [ ]
- [ ]
- [ ]
- [ ]
- [ ]

> "Never think that what you have to offer is insignificant. There will always be someone out there that needs what you have to give."

DATE _____

WRITING GOALS

....
....
....
....
....
....
....
....
....
....

BLOGGING GOALS

....
....
....
....
....
....
....

SOCIAL MEDIA GOALS

f

....
....
....
....

t

....
....
....
....

IG

....
....
....
....

P

....
....
....
....

> "Without strategy, content is just stuff, and the world has enough stuff."
>
> ~ @arjunbasu

IMPORTANT ACTIVITIES FOR TODAY

- [ ] ....
- [ ] ....
- [ ] ....
- [ ] ....
- [ ] ....
- [ ] ....
- [ ] ....
- [ ] ....

DATE _____

SOCIAL MEDIA GOALS

WRITING GOALS

BLOGGING GOALS

IMPORTANT ACTIVITIES FOR TODAY

- [ ]
- [ ]
- [ ]
- [ ]
- [ ]
- [ ]
- [ ]
- [ ]

"Marketing is enthusiasm transferred to the customer."

~Gregory Cio

DATE _____

WRITING GOALS

SOCIAL MEDIA GOALS

BLOGGING GOALS

IMPORTANT ACTIVITIES FOR TODAY

- [ ]
- [ ]
- [ ]
- [ ]
- [ ]
- [ ]
- [ ]
- [ ]

> "People do not buy goods and services. They buy relations, stories and magic."
>
> ~Seth Godin

DATE _____

SOCIAL MEDIA GOALS

WRITING GOALS

BLOGGING GOALS

IMPORTANT ACTIVITIES FOR TODAY

- [ ]
- [ ]
- [ ]
- [ ]
- [ ]
- [ ]
- [ ]
- [ ]

"Stop selling, start helping."

~Zig Zigler

DATE _____

	MONDAY	TUESDAY	WEDNESDAY
☐			
☐			
☐			
☐			
☐			

DATE _____

THURSDAY	FRIDAY	SATURDAY / SUNDAY
☐	☐	☐
☐	☐	☐
☐	☐	☐
☐	☐	☐
☐	☐	☐

DATE _____

Newsletter Thoughts

DATE _____

Book Promotion Plans

DATE _____

WRITING GOALS

SOCIAL MEDIA GOALS

BLOGGING GOALS

IMPORTANT ACTIVITIES FOR TODAY

- [ ]
- [ ]
- [ ]
- [ ]
- [ ]
- [ ]
- [ ]
- [ ]

> "Marketing is no longer about the stuff yo make, but about the stories you tell."
> ~Seth Godin

DATE _____

SOCIAL MEDIA GOALS

WRITING GOALS

BLOGGING GOALS

IMPORTANT ACTIVITIES FOR TODAY

- [ ]
- [ ]
- [ ]
- [ ]
- [ ]
- [ ]
- [ ]
- [ ]

> "Don't deliver a Product – Deliver an Experience."

DATE _____

WRITING GOALS

BLOGGING GOALS

SOCIAL MEDIA GOALS

Facebook

Twitter

Instagram

Pinterest

> "Strive not to be a success, but rather to be of value."
> ~Albert Einstein

IMPORTANT ACTIVITIES FOR TODAY

- [ ]
- [ ]
- [ ]
- [ ]
- [ ]
- [ ]
- [ ]
- [ ]

DATE _____

SOCIAL MEDIA GOALS

[Facebook]

....
....
....
....

[Twitter]

....
....
....
....

[Instagram]

....
....
....
....

[Pinterest]

....
....
....
....

WRITING GOALS

....
....
....
....
....
....
....
....
....
....
....
....

BLOGGING GOALS

....
....
....
....
....
....
....
....

IMPORTANT ACTIVITIES FOR TODAY

- [ ] ....
- [ ] ....
- [ ] ....
- [ ] ....
- [ ] ....
- [ ] ....
- [ ] ....
- [ ] ....

"Be a resource, not a sales pitch."

DATE _____

WRITING GOALS

....
....
....
....
....
....
....
....
....
....

BLOGGING GOALS

....
....
....
....
....
....
....

SOCIAL MEDIA GOALS

f
....
....
....
....

t
....
....
....
....

ig
....
....
....
....

p
....
....
....
....

> "The best marketing strategy ever: CARE."
> ~Gary Vaynerchuk

IMPORTANT ACTIVITIES FOR TODAY

- [ ] ....
- [ ] ....
- [ ] ....
- [ ] ....
- [ ] ....
- [ ] ....
- [ ] ....
- [ ] ....
- [ ] ....

DATE _____

SOCIAL MEDIA GOALS

f

....
....
....
....

🐦

....
....
....
....

📷

....
....
....
....

P

....
....
....
....

WRITING GOALS

....
....
....
....
....
....
....
....
....
....

BLOGGING GOALS

....
....
....
....
....
....
....

IMPORTANT ACTIVITIES FOR TODAY

- [ ] ....
- [ ] ....
- [ ] ....
- [ ] ....
- [ ] ....
- [ ] ....
- [ ] ....
- [ ] ....

"Branding is what people say about you when you are not in the room."

DATE _____

WRITING GOALS

SOCIAL MEDIA GOALS

BLOGGING GOALS

IMPORTANT ACTIVITIES FOR TODAY

- [ ]
- [ ]
- [ ]
- [ ]
- [ ]
- [ ]
- [ ]
- [ ]

"Marketing without data is like driving with your eyes closed."

~Dan Zarella

DATE _____

SOCIAL MEDIA GOALS

WRITING GOALS

BLOGGING GOALS

IMPORTANT ACTIVITIES FOR TODAY

- [ ]
- [ ]
- [ ]
- [ ]
- [ ]
- [ ]
- [ ]
- [ ]

"Everyone is not your customer."

~Seth Godin

DATE _____

WRITING GOALS

BLOGGING GOALS

SOCIAL MEDIA GOALS

IMPORTANT ACTIVITIES FOR TODAY

- [ ]
- [ ]
- [ ]
- [ ]
- [ ]
- [ ]
- [ ]
- [ ]

> "To give real service, you must add something which cannot be bought or measured with money, and that is sincerity and integrity."
>
> ~Douglas Adams

DATE _____

SOCIAL MEDIA GOALS

WRITING GOALS

BLOGGING GOALS

IMPORTANT ACTIVITIES FOR TODAY

"Content is fire, Social Media is gasoline."

~Jay Baer

DATE _____

WRITING GOALS

SOCIAL MEDIA GOALS

BLOGGING GOALS

IMPORTANT ACTIVITIES FOR TODAY

"The best advertising you can have is a loyal customer spreading the word about how incredible your business is."

~Shep Hyken

DATE _____

SOCIAL MEDIA GOALS

f
....
....
....
....

t
....
....
....
....

◉
....
....
....
....

P
....
....
....
....

WRITING GOALS

....
....
....
....
....
....
....
....
....
....
....
....

BLOGGING GOALS

....
....
....
....
....
....
....

IMPORTANT ACTIVITIES FOR TODAY

☐ ....
☐ ....
☐ ....
☐ ....
☐ ....
☐ ....
☐ ....
☐ ....

> "Supporting another's success won't ever dampen yours."

DATE _____

WRITING GOALS

....
....
....
....
....
....
....
....
....

BLOGGING GOALS

....
....
....
....
....
....
....

SOCIAL MEDIA GOALS

f
....
....
....

t
....
....
....

📷
....
....
....

P
....
....
....

"Maybe don't call it social media. Just be human and tell your story."
~Gary Vaynerchuck

IMPORTANT ACTIVITIES FOR TODAY

☐ ....
☐ ....
☐ ....
☐ ....
☐ ....
☐ ....
☐ ....
☐ ....

DATE _____

SOCIAL MEDIA GOALS

f
....
....
....
....

t
....
....
....
....

ig
....
....
....
....

p
....
....
....
....

WRITING GOALS

....
....
....
....
....
....
....
....

BLOGGING GOALS

....
....
....
....
....
....
....

IMPORTANT ACTIVITIES FOR TODAY

- [ ] ....
- [ ] ....
- [ ] ....
- [ ] ....
- [ ] ....
- [ ] ....
- [ ] ....
- [ ] ....

> "Google only loves you when everyone else loves you first."
>
> ~Wendy Piersall

DATE _____

WRITING GOALS

SOCIAL MEDIA GOALS

BLOGGING GOALS

> "Consumers do not buy products. They buy product benefits."
>
> ~David Ogilvy

IMPORTANT ACTIVITIES FOR TODAY

- [ ]
- [ ]
- [ ]
- [ ]
- [ ]
- [ ]
- [ ]
- [ ]

DATE _____

SOCIAL MEDIA GOALS

f
....
....
....
....

t
....
....
....
....

ig
....
....
....
....

p
....
....
....
....

WRITING GOALS

....
....
....
....
....
....
....
....
....

BLOGGING GOALS

....
....
....
....
....
....
....
....

IMPORTANT ACTIVITIES FOR TODAY

☐
☐
☐
☐
☐
☐
☐
☐

"Leadership is the ability to hide your panic from others."

~Lao Tuz

DATE _____

WRITING GOALS

SOCIAL MEDIA GOALS

BLOGGING GOALS

IMPORTANT ACTIVITIES FOR TODAY

- [ ]
- [ ]
- [ ]
- [ ]
- [ ]
- [ ]
- [ ]
- [ ]

"You have to learn the rules of the game and then you have to play better than anyone else."

~Albert Einstein

DATE _____

SOCIAL MEDIA GOALS

Facebook
....
....
....
....

Twitter
....
....
....
....

Instagram
....
....
....
....

Pinterest
....
....
....
....

WRITING GOALS
....
....
....
....
....
....
....
....
....
....

BLOGGING GOALS
....
....
....
....
....
....
....

IMPORTANT ACTIVITIES FOR TODAY
- [ ] ....
- [ ] ....
- [ ] ....
- [ ] ....
- [ ] ....
- [ ] ....
- [ ] ....
- [ ] ....

> "If you want something you never had, you need to do something you've never done."

DATE _____

WRITING GOALS

SOCIAL MEDIA GOALS

BLOGGING GOALS

"Sell the problem you solve, not the product."

~Zac Efron

IMPORTANT ACTIVITIES FOR TODAY

☐
☐
☐
☐
☐
☐
☐
☐

DATE _____

SOCIAL MEDIA GOALS

Facebook

....
....
....
....

Twitter

....
....
....
....

Instagram

....
....
....
....

Pinterest

....
....
....
....

WRITING GOALS

....
....
....
....
....
....
....
....
....
....
....

BLOGGING GOALS

....
....
....
....
....
....

IMPORTANT ACTIVITIES FOR TODAY

- [ ] ....
- [ ] ....
- [ ] ....
- [ ] ....
- [ ] ....
- [ ] ....
- [ ] ....
- [ ] ....

> "If someone offers you an amazing opportunity and you're not sure you can do it, say yes – then learn how to do it later."
>
> ~Richard Branson

DATE _____

WRITING GOALS

....
....
....
....
....
....
....
....
....
....

SOCIAL MEDIA GOALS

f
....
....
....
....

🐦
....
....
....
....

📷
....
....
....
....

BLOGGING GOALS

....
....
....
....
....
....

P
....
....
....
....

> "The best marketing doesn't feel like marketing"
> ~Tom Fishbourne

IMPORTANT ACTIVITIES FOR TODAY

- [ ] ....
- [ ] ....
- [ ] ....
- [ ] ....
- [ ] ....
- [ ] ....
- [ ] ....
- [ ] ....
- [ ] ....

DATE _____

SOCIAL MEDIA GOALS

[Facebook]
....
....
....
....

[Twitter]
....
....
....
....

[Instagram]
....
....
....
....

[Pinterest]
....
....
....
....

WRITING GOALS

....
....
....
....
....
....
....
....
....

BLOGGING GOALS

....
....
....
....
....
....
....

IMPORTANT ACTIVITIES FOR TODAY

- [ ] ....
- [ ] ....
- [ ] ....
- [ ] ....
- [ ] ....
- [ ] ....
- [ ] ....
- [ ] ....

> "Advertising is saying you're good. PR is getting someone else to say you're good."
>
> ~Jean-Louis Gassee

DATE _____

WRITING GOALS

....
....
....
....
....
....
....
....
....
....

BLOGGING GOALS

....
....
....
....
....
....
....

SOCIAL MEDIA GOALS

f
....
....
....
....

t
....
....
....
....

ig
....
....
....

p
....
....
....

> "Either write something worth reading or do something worth writing."
> ~Benjamin Franklin

IMPORTANT ACTIVITIES FOR TODAY

- [ ] ....
- [ ] ....
- [ ] ....
- [ ] ....
- [ ] ....
- [ ] ....
- [ ] ....
- [ ] ....

DATE _____

SOCIAL MEDIA GOALS

WRITING GOALS

BLOGGING GOALS

IMPORTANT ACTIVITIES FOR TODAY

- [ ]
- [ ]
- [ ]
- [ ]
- [ ]
- [ ]
- [ ]
- [ ]

> "If you don't track your visits and visitors on your website then how can you tell if your social media presence is actually making a difference?"
>
> ~Ian Anderson Gray

DATE _____

WRITING GOALS

SOCIAL MEDIA GOALS

BLOGGING GOALS

IMPORTANT ACTIVITIES FOR TODAY

- [ ]
- [ ]
- [ ]
- [ ]
- [ ]
- [ ]
- [ ]
- [ ]

> "The goal of social media is to turn customers into a volunteer marketing army."
>
> ~Jay Baer

DATE _____

SOCIAL MEDIA GOALS

f

t

IG

P

WRITING GOALS

BLOGGING GOALS

IMPORTANT ACTIVITIES FOR TODAY

- [ ]
- [ ]
- [ ]
- [ ]
- [ ]
- [ ]
- [ ]
- [ ]
- [ ]

"When you say it – it's marketing. When they say it – its social proof."

~Andy Crestodina

DATE _____

WRITING GOALS

....
....
....
....
....
....
....
....
....
....
....
....

BLOGGING GOALS

....
....
....
....
....
....
....

SOCIAL MEDIA GOALS

f
....
....
....
....

t
....
....
....
....

ig
....
....
....
....

p
....
....
....

> "The best content spreads by itself."
> ~Brian Clark

IMPORTANT ACTIVITIES FOR TODAY

- [ ] ....
- [ ] ....
- [ ] ....
- [ ] ....
- [ ] ....
- [ ] ....
- [ ] ....
- [ ] ....

DATE _____

SOCIAL MEDIA GOALS

Facebook
....
....
....
....

Twitter
....
....
....
....

Instagram
....
....
....
....

Pinterest
....
....
....
....

WRITING GOALS

....
....
....
....
....
....
....
....
....
....

BLOGGING GOALS

....
....
....
....
....
....
....

IMPORTANT ACTIVITIES FOR TODAY

- [ ] ....
- [ ] ....
- [ ] ....
- [ ] ....
- [ ] ....
- [ ] ....
- [ ] ....
- [ ] ....

> "Kids are using social media the RIGHT way. They are using it to communicate."
>
> ~Ted Rubin

DATE _____

WRITING GOALS

BLOGGING GOALS

SOCIAL MEDIA GOALS

IMPORTANT ACTIVITIES FOR TODAY

- [ ]
- [ ]
- [ ]
- [ ]
- [ ]
- [ ]
- [ ]
- [ ]

"If what you are saying doesn't add value they won't listen to you.

~Marcus Sheridan

DATE _____

SOCIAL MEDIA GOALS

f
....
....
....
....

🐦
....
....
....
....

📷
....
....
....
....

P
....
....
....
....

WRITING GOALS

....
....
....
....
....
....
....
....
....
....

BLOGGING GOALS

....
....
....
....
....
....
....
....

IMPORTANT ACTIVITIES FOR TODAY

- [ ] ....
- [ ] ....
- [ ] ....
- [ ] ....
- [ ] ....
- [ ] ....
- [ ] ....
- [ ] ....

> "Never build your content ship on rented land."
>
> ~Joe Pulizzi

DATE _____

MONDAY	TUESDAY	WEDNESDAY
☐	☐	☐
☐	☐	☐
☐	☐	☐
☐	☐	☐
☐	☐	☐

DATE _____

THURSDAY	FRIDAY	SATURDAY / SUNDAY
☐	☐	☐
☐	☐	☐
☐	☐	☐
☐	☐	☐
☐	☐	☐

DATE _____

Newsletter Thoughts

DATE _____

Book Promotion Plans

DATE _____

WRITING GOALS

....
....
....
....
....
....
....
....
....
....
....

BLOGGING GOALS

....
....
....
....
....
....
....
....

SOCIAL MEDIA GOALS

f
....
....
....
....

t
....
....
....
....

ig
....
....
....
....

p
....
....
....
....

> "Content that helps is superior to content that sells."
> ~Jay Baer

IMPORTANT ACTIVITIES FOR TODAY

- [ ] ....
- [ ] ....
- [ ] ....
- [ ] ....
- [ ] ....
- [ ] ....
- [ ] ....
- [ ] ....

DATE _____

SOCIAL MEDIA GOALS

WRITING GOALS

BLOGGING GOALS

IMPORTANT ACTIVITIES FOR TODAY

- [ ]
- [ ]
- [ ]
- [ ]
- [ ]
- [ ]
- [ ]
- [ ]

> "We are in the business of listening, communicating, teaching and helping."
>
> ~Marcus Sheridan

DATE _____

WRITING GOALS

SOCIAL MEDIA GOALS

BLOGGING GOALS

IMPORTANT ACTIVITIES FOR TODAY

- [ ]
- [ ]
- [ ]
- [ ]
- [ ]
- [ ]
- [ ]
- [ ]

> "Power doesn't come from CONTENT, power comes from content that MOVES.
>
> ~Mark Schaefer

DATE _____

SOCIAL MEDIA GOALS

f
....
....
....
....

🐦
....
....
....
....

📷
....
....
....
....

P
....
....
....
....

WRITING GOALS

....
....
....
....
....
....
....
....
....

BLOGGING GOALS

....
....
....
....
....
....
....

IMPORTANT ACTIVITIES FOR TODAY

- [ ] ....
- [ ] ....
- [ ] ....
- [ ] ....
- [ ] ....
- [ ] ....
- [ ] ....
- [ ] ....

> "Find your sweet spot: the intersection between what you know & what your customers need to know."
>
> ~Joe Pulizzi

DATE _____

WRITING GOALS

BLOGGING GOALS

SOCIAL MEDIA GOALS

IMPORTANT ACTIVITIES FOR TODAY

- [ ]
- [ ]
- [ ]
- [ ]
- [ ]
- [ ]
- [ ]
- [ ]

"Ask what you can do for influencers, not what influencers can do for you – develop relationships!

~Laura Fitton

DATE _____

SOCIAL MEDIA GOALS

WRITING GOALS

BLOGGING GOALS

IMPORTANT ACTIVITIES FOR TODAY

- [ ]
- [ ]
- [ ]
- [ ]
- [ ]
- [ ]
- [ ]
- [ ]

> "When you connect with influencers and use their content, you build your own influence as well."
>
> ~Lee Odden

DATE _____

WRITING GOALS

BLOGGING GOALS

SOCIAL MEDIA GOALS

"Lead with a personal story. Give your audience a way to connect and show you're a real person.

~Michael Hyatt

IMPORTANT ACTIVITIES FOR TODAY

- [ ]
- [ ]
- [ ]
- [ ]
- [ ]
- [ ]
- [ ]
- [ ]
- [ ]

DATE _____

SOCIAL MEDIA GOALS

f
....
....
....
....

🐦
....
....
....
....

📷
....
....
....
....

P
....
....
....
....

WRITING GOALS

....
....
....
....
....
....
....
....
....

BLOGGING GOALS

....
....
....
....
....
....

IMPORTANT ACTIVITIES FOR TODAY

- [ ] ....
- [ ] ....
- [ ] ....
- [ ] ....
- [ ] ....
- [ ] ....
- [ ] ....
- [ ] ....

> "Relationships are like muscle tissue, the more they are engaged, the stronger and more valuable they become."
>
> ~Ted Rubin

DATE

WRITING GOALS

BLOGGING GOALS

SOCIAL MEDIA GOALS

IMPORTANT ACTIVITIES FOR TODAY

- [ ]
- [ ]
- [ ]
- [ ]
- [ ]
- [ ]
- [ ]
- [ ]

"Whoever generates the most trust on-line wins."

~Marcus Sheridan

DATE _____

SOCIAL MEDIA GOALS

Facebook

....
....
....
....

Twitter

....
....
....
....

Instagram

....
....
....
....

Pinterest

....
....
....
....

WRITING GOALS

....
....
....
....
....
....
....
....
....
....

BLOGGING GOALS

....
....
....
....
....
....

IMPORTANT ACTIVITIES FOR TODAY

- [ ] ....
- [ ] ....
- [ ] ....
- [ ] ....
- [ ] ....
- [ ] ....
- [ ] ....
- [ ] ....

> "When finished writing a post, go back & add bullets, sub heads, spacing; eliminate long paragraphs or sentences."
>
> ~Michael Hyatt

DATE _____

WRITING GOALS

....
....
....
....
....
....
....
....
....

SOCIAL MEDIA GOALS

f
....
....
....
....

t
....
....
....
....

[instagram]
....
....
....

p
....
....
....

BLOGGING GOALS

....
....
....
....
....
....

IMPORTANT ACTIVITIES FOR TODAY

☐ ....
☐ ....
☐ ....
☐ ....
☐ ....
☐ ....
☐ ....
☐ ....
☐ ....

DATE _____

SOCIAL MEDIA GOALS

[Facebook]
....
....
....
....

[Twitter]
....
....
....
....

[Instagram]
....
....
....
....

[Pinterest]
....
....
....
....

WRITING GOALS

....
....
....
....
....
....
....
....
....
....

BLOGGING GOALS

....
....
....
....
....
....
....
....

IMPORTANT ACTIVITIES FOR TODAY

- [ ] ....
- [ ] ....
- [ ] ....
- [ ] ....
- [ ] ....
- [ ] ....
- [ ] ....
- [ ] ....

> "Social media is not an end in itself. It's just another tool to reach people."
>
> ~Simon Mainwaring

DATE

WRITING GOALS

BLOGGING GOALS

SOCIAL MEDIA GOALS

IMPORTANT ACTIVITIES FOR TODAY

- [ ]
- [ ]
- [ ]
- [ ]
- [ ]
- [ ]
- [ ]
- [ ]

> "Social media policies will never be able to cure stupid."
> ~Nichole Kelly

DATE _____

SOCIAL MEDIA GOALS

f

t

◉

P

WRITING GOALS

BLOGGING GOALS

IMPORTANT ACTIVITIES FOR TODAY

- ☐
- ☐
- ☐
- ☐
- ☐
- ☐
- ☐
- ☐

> "Saying hello doesn't have an ROI. It's about building relationships."
>
> ~Gary Vaynerchuk

DATE _____

WRITING GOALS

SOCIAL MEDIA GOALS

BLOGGING GOALS

IMPORTANT ACTIVITIES FOR TODAY

- [ ]
- [ ]
- [ ]
- [ ]
- [ ]
- [ ]
- [ ]
- [ ]

"Be selective. Just because a particular social media channel exists doesn't mean it's right for your business."

~markarmstrongillustrations.com

DATE _____

SOCIAL MEDIA GOALS

f
....
....
....
....

t
....
....
....
....

ig
....
....
....
....

p
....
....
....
....

WRITING GOALS

....
....
....
....
....
....
....
....
....
....

BLOGGING GOALS

....
....
....
....
....
....
....

IMPORTANT ACTIVITIES FOR TODAY

- [ ] ....
- [ ] ....
- [ ] ....
- [ ] ....
- [ ] ....
- [ ] ....
- [ ] ....
- [ ] ....
- [ ] ....

> "Social media creates communities, not markets."
>
> ~Don Schultz

DATE _____

WRITING GOALS

SOCIAL MEDIA GOALS

BLOGGING GOALS

> "Only one mode of communication with your ideal prospects remains steadfast in the face of a changing social media landscape – Email."
>
> ~Amy Porterfield

IMPORTANT ACTIVITIES FOR TODAY

- [ ]
- [ ]
- [ ]
- [ ]
- [ ]
- [ ]
- [ ]
- [ ]

DATE _____

SOCIAL MEDIA GOALS

f

t

IG

P

WRITING GOALS

BLOGGING GOALS

IMPORTANT ACTIVITIES FOR TODAY

- [ ]
- [ ]
- [ ]
- [ ]
- [ ]
- [ ]
- [ ]
- [ ]

> "Learn from those that are getting results and model what's already working."
>
> ~Amy Porterfield

DATE _____

WRITING GOALS

BLOGGING GOALS

SOCIAL MEDIA GOALS

f

🐦

📷

P

"Take Action daily to move your business forward."

~Amy Porterfield

IMPORTANT ACTIVITIES FOR TODAY

- [ ]
- [ ]
- [ ]
- [ ]
- [ ]
- [ ]
- [ ]
- [ ]
- [ ]

DATE _____

SOCIAL MEDIA GOALS

f
....
....
....
....

Twitter
....
....
....
....

Instagram
....
....
....
....

Pinterest
....
....
....
....

WRITING GOALS

....
....
....
....
....
....
....
....
....
....

BLOGGING GOALS

....
....
....
....
....
....

IMPORTANT ACTIVITIES FOR TODAY

- [ ] ....
- [ ] ....
- [ ] ....
- [ ] ....
- [ ] ....
- [ ] ....
- [ ] ....
- [ ] ....

> "I like to say that Twitter is like a bar, Facebook is your living room and LinkedIn is the local chamber of commerce."
>
> ~BSStoltz

DATE _____

WRITING GOALS

SOCIAL MEDIA GOALS

BLOGGING GOALS

IMPORTANT ACTIVITIES FOR TODAY

- [ ]
- [ ]
- [ ]
- [ ]
- [ ]
- [ ]
- [ ]
- [ ]
- [ ]

> "There are THREE sides to every online interaction: Yours, mine and the view of everyone watching us. Act carefully."
>
> ~Mack Collier

DATE _____

SOCIAL MEDIA GOALS

[Facebook]
....
....
....
....

[Twitter]
....
....
....
....

[Instagram]
....
....
....
....

[Pinterest]
....
....
....
....

WRITING GOALS

....
....
....
....
....
....
....
....
....
....

BLOGGING GOALS

....
....
....
....
....
....
....

IMPORTANT ACTIVITIES FOR TODAY

- [ ] ....
- [ ] ....
- [ ] ....
- [ ] ....
- [ ] ....
- [ ] ....
- [ ] ....
- [ ] ....

> "Social media is a lot like the dating process. I want flowers and chocolates and all the fun repartee that goes along with a new relationship."
>
> ~Rebekah Radice

DATE _____

WRITING GOALS

SOCIAL MEDIA GOALS

BLOGGING GOALS

IMPORTANT ACTIVITIES FOR TODAY

- [ ]
- [ ]
- [ ]
- [ ]
- [ ]
- [ ]
- [ ]
- [ ]

"No matter what people tell you, words and ideas can change the world."

~ Robin Williams

DATE _____

SOCIAL MEDIA GOALS

f
....
....
....
....

t
....
....
....
....

IG
....
....
....
....

P
....
....
....
....

WRITING GOALS

....
....
....
....
....
....
....
....
....
....

BLOGGING GOALS

....
....
....
....
....
....
....
....

IMPORTANT ACTIVITIES FOR TODAY

- [ ] ....
- [ ] ....
- [ ] ....
- [ ] ....
- [ ] ....
- [ ] ....
- [ ] ....
- [ ] ....

> "Social tools are not just about giving people a voice, but giving them a way to collaborate, contribute and connect."
>
> ~John Stepper

DATE _____

WRITING GOALS

SOCIAL MEDIA GOALS

BLOGGING GOALS

IMPORTANT ACTIVITIES FOR TODAY

- [ ]
- [ ]
- [ ]
- [ ]
- [ ]
- [ ]
- [ ]
- [ ]

> "You can be professional while also keeping it real with your customers, by interacting with customers in a less formal way, you'll build a strong human connection that helps build brand loyalty."
>
> ~David Hauser

DATE _____

SOCIAL MEDIA GOALS

WRITING GOALS

BLOGGING GOALS

IMPORTANT ACTIVITIES FOR TODAY

- [ ]
- [ ]
- [ ]
- [ ]
- [ ]
- [ ]
- [ ]
- [ ]

> "Don't focus on having a great blog. Focus on producing a blog that's good for your readers."
>
> ~Brian Clark

DATE _____

WRITING GOALS

....
....
....
....
....
....
....
....
....
....

BLOGGING GOALS

....
....
....
....
....
....
....

SOCIAL MEDIA GOALS

f
....
....
....
....

t
....
....
....
....

ig
....
....
....
....

p
....
....
....
....

> "As a blogger, everything that you do flows from understanding your audience and seeking to help them as much as possible."
>
> ~Brian Clark

IMPORTANT ACTIVITIES FOR TODAY

☐ ....
☐ ....
☐ ....
☐ ....
☐ ....
☐ ....
☐ ....
☐ ....

DATE _____

SOCIAL MEDIA GOALS

WRITING GOALS

BLOGGING GOALS

IMPORTANT ACTIVITIES FOR TODAY

- [ ]
- [ ]
- [ ]
- [ ]
- [ ]
- [ ]
- [ ]
- [ ]

"Blogging is a conversation, not a quote."

~Mike Butcher

DATE _____

WRITING GOALS

SOCIAL MEDIA GOALS

BLOGGING GOALS

IMPORTANT ACTIVITIES FOR TODAY

- [ ]
- [ ]
- [ ]
- [ ]
- [ ]
- [ ]
- [ ]
- [ ]

> "Blogging is only as interesting as the interest shown in others."
> ~Lee Odden

DATE _____

SOCIAL MEDIA GOALS

WRITING GOALS

BLOGGING GOALS

IMPORTANT ACTIVITIES FOR TODAY

- [ ]
- [ ]
- [ ]
- [ ]
- [ ]
- [ ]
- [ ]
- [ ]
- [ ]

> "Blogging is just writing – writing using a particularly efficient type of publishing technology."
>
> ~Simon Dumenco

DATE _____

WRITING GOALS

SOCIAL MEDIA GOALS

BLOGGING GOALS

> "Blogging is to writing what extreme sports are to athletics: more free-form, more accident-prone, less formal, more alive. It is, in many ways, writing out loud."
>
> ~Andrew Sullivan

IMPORTANT ACTIVITIES FOR TODAY

- [ ]
- [ ]
- [ ]
- [ ]
- [ ]
- [ ]
- [ ]
- [ ]

DATE _____

SOCIAL MEDIA GOALS

f
....
....
....
....

🐦
....
....
....
....

📷
....
....
....
....

P
....
....
....
....

WRITING GOALS

....
....
....
....
....
....
....
....
....
....

BLOGGING GOALS

....
....
....
....
....
....
....

IMPORTANT ACTIVITIES FOR TODAY

- [ ] ....
- [ ] ....
- [ ] ....
- [ ] ....
- [ ] ....
- [ ] ....
- [ ] ....
- [ ] ....

> "In the last decade, blogging has turned the publishing world on its head. A blog allows you to write and publish anything, from anywhere, and have it be immediately available to billions of people all around the world."
>
> ~Andrew Sullivan

DATE _____

WRITING GOALS

SOCIAL MEDIA GOALS

BLOGGING GOALS

IMPORTANT ACTIVITIES FOR TODAY

- [ ]
- [ ]
- [ ]
- [ ]
- [ ]
- [ ]
- [ ]
- [ ]

> "Blogging is a communication mechanism handed to us by the long tail of the internet."
> ~Tom Foremski

DATE _____

SOCIAL MEDIA GOALS

WRITING GOALS

BLOGGING GOALS

IMPORTANT ACTIVITIES FOR TODAY

- [ ]
- [ ]
- [ ]
- [ ]
- [ ]
- [ ]
- [ ]
- [ ]

> "The first thing you need to decide when you build your blog is what you want to accomplish with it, and what it can do if successful."
>
> ~Ron Dawson

DATE _____

WRITING GOALS

....
....
....
....
....
....
....
....

SOCIAL MEDIA GOALS

[Facebook]
....
....
....
....

[Twitter]
....
....
....
....

[Instagram]
....
....
....
....

BLOGGING GOALS

....
....
....
....
....
....

[Pinterest]
....
....
....
....

> "Don't try to plan everything out to the very last detail. I'm a big believer in just getting it out there: Create a minimal viable product or website, launch it, and get feedback."
>
> ~Neil Patel

IMPORTANT ACTIVITIES FOR TODAY

- [ ] ....
- [ ] ....
- [ ] ....
- [ ] ....
- [ ] ....
- [ ] ....
- [ ] ....
- [ ] ....

DATE _____

SOCIAL MEDIA GOALS

[f]
....
....
....
....

[twitter]
....
....
....
....

[instagram]
....
....
....
....

[pinterest]
....
....
....
....

WRITING GOALS

....
....
....
....
....
....
....
....
....
....
....
....

BLOGGING GOALS

....
....
....
....
....
....
....

IMPORTANT ACTIVITIES FOR TODAY

- [ ] ....
- [ ] ....
- [ ] ....
- [ ] ....
- [ ] ....
- [ ] ....
- [ ] ....
- [ ] ....

> "The casual conversational tone of a blog is what makes it particularly dangerous."
>
> ~Daniel B. Beaulieu

DATE _____

MONDAY	TUESDAY	WEDNESDAY
☐	☐	☐
☐	☐	☐
☐	☐	☐
☐	☐	☐
☐	☐	☐

DATE _____

THURSDAY	FRIDAY	SATURDAY / SUNDAY
☐	☐	☐
☐	☐	☐
☐	☐	☐
☐	☐	☐
☐	☐	☐

DATE _____

Newsletter Thoughts

DATE _____

Book Promotion Plans

DATE _____

WRITING GOALS

BLOGGING GOALS

SOCIAL MEDIA GOALS

IMPORTANT ACTIVITIES FOR TODAY

- [ ]
- [ ]
- [ ]
- [ ]
- [ ]
- [ ]
- [ ]
- [ ]

> "Not only are bloggers suckers for the remarkable, so are the people who read blogs."
>
> ~Seth Godin

DATE _____

SOCIAL MEDIA GOALS

WRITING GOALS

BLOGGING GOALS

IMPORTANT ACTIVITIES FOR TODAY

- [ ]
- [ ]
- [ ]
- [ ]
- [ ]
- [ ]
- [ ]
- [ ]

> "When you write remarkable content, you stay engaged and excited with your blog. Your readers follow suit."
>
> ~Seth Godin

DATE _____

WRITING GOALS

....
....
....
....
....
....
....
....
....
....

BLOGGING GOALS

....
....
....
....
....
....
....
....

SOCIAL MEDIA GOALS

[Facebook]
....
....
....
....

[Twitter]
....
....
....
....

[Instagram]
....
....
....
....

[Pinterest]
....
....
....
....

> "Where the Internet is about availability of information, blogging is about making information creation available to anyone."
>
> ~George Siemens

IMPORTANT ACTIVITIES FOR TODAY

- [ ] ....
- [ ] ....
- [ ] ....
- [ ] ....
- [ ] ....
- [ ] ....
- [ ] ....
- [ ] ....

DATE _____

SOCIAL MEDIA GOALS

[Facebook]

[Twitter]

[Instagram]

[Pinterest]

WRITING GOALS

BLOGGING GOALS

IMPORTANT ACTIVITIES FOR TODAY

- [ ]
- [ ]
- [ ]
- [ ]
- [ ]
- [ ]
- [ ]
- [ ]

> "There are tons of different factors that go into ranking well, but the biggest is high-quality content."
>
> ~David Sinick

DATE _____

WRITING GOALS

SOCIAL MEDIA GOALS

Facebook

Twitter

Instagram

Pinterest

BLOGGING GOALS

IMPORTANT ACTIVITIES FOR TODAY

- [ ]
- [ ]
- [ ]
- [ ]
- [ ]
- [ ]
- [ ]
- [ ]
- [ ]

> "Your ultimate consumers are your users, not search engines."
>
> ~Google's SEO Starter Guide

DATE _____

SOCIAL MEDIA GOALS

f
....
....
....
....

t
....
....
....
....

ig
....
....
....
....

p
....
....
....
....

WRITING GOALS

....
....
....
....
....
....
....
....
....

BLOGGING GOALS

....
....
....
....
....
....
....

IMPORTANT ACTIVITIES FOR TODAY

- [ ] ....
- [ ] ....
- [ ] ....
- [ ] ....
- [ ] ....
- [ ] ....
- [ ] ....
- [ ] ....

> "Blogging is hard because of the grind required to stay interesting and relevant."
>
> ~Sufia Tippu

DATE _____

WRITING GOALS

SOCIAL MEDIA GOALS

[f]

[t]

[ig]

BLOGGING GOALS

[p]

> "If you want to continually grow your blog, you need to learn to blog on a consistent basis."
>
> ~Neil Patel

IMPORTANT ACTIVITIES FOR TODAY

- [ ]
- [ ]
- [ ]
- [ ]
- [ ]
- [ ]
- [ ]
- [ ]
- [ ]

DATE _____

SOCIAL MEDIA GOALS

f

t

IG

P

WRITING GOALS

BLOGGING GOALS

IMPORTANT ACTIVITIES FOR TODAY

- [ ]
- [ ]
- [ ]
- [ ]
- [ ]
- [ ]
- [ ]
- [ ]

> "You can work quite hard, in particular online, and do quite well independently, but if you really want to grow you need points of leverage and most of them come from knowing people."
>
> ~Yaro Starak

DATE _____

WRITING GOALS

BLOGGING GOALS

SOCIAL MEDIA GOALS

IMPORTANT ACTIVITIES FOR TODAY

- [ ]
- [ ]
- [ ]
- [ ]
- [ ]
- [ ]
- [ ]
- [ ]

> "If you love writing or making music or blogging or any sort of performing art, then do it. Do it with everything you've got. Just don't plan on using it as a shortcut to making a living."
>
> ~Seth Godin

DATE _____

SOCIAL MEDIA GOALS

f
....
....
....
....

🐦
....
....
....
....

📷
....
....
....
....

P
....
....
....
....

WRITING GOALS

....
....
....
....
....
....
....
....
....
....
....
....

BLOGGING GOALS

....
....
....
....
....
....
....

IMPORTANT ACTIVITIES FOR TODAY

- [ ] ....
- [ ] ....
- [ ] ....
- [ ] ....
- [ ] ....
- [ ] ....
- [ ] ....
- [ ] ....

> "Social media is not a fad because it's human."
>
> ~Gary Vaynerchuk

DATE _____

WRITING GOALS

....
....
....
....
....
....
....
....
....
....

BLOGGING GOALS

....
....
....
....
....
....
....
....

SOCIAL MEDIA GOALS

f
....
....
....
....

t
....
....
....
....

○
....
....
....
....

p
....
....
....
....

> "Successful blogging is not about one time hits. It's about building a loyal following over time."
> ~David Aston

IMPORTANT ACTIVITIES FOR TODAY

- [ ] ....
- [ ] ....
- [ ] ....
- [ ] ....
- [ ] ....
- [ ] ....
- [ ] ....
- [ ] ....

DATE _____

SOCIAL MEDIA GOALS

WRITING GOALS

BLOGGING GOALS

IMPORTANT ACTIVITIES FOR TODAY

- [ ]
- [ ]
- [ ]
- [ ]
- [ ]
- [ ]
- [ ]
- [ ]

> "There's a lot of information out there for free, so you've got to figure out what makes your information different."
>
> ~Matt Wolfe

DATE _____

WRITING GOALS

SOCIAL MEDIA GOALS

f

t

ig

p

BLOGGING GOALS

> "What you do after you create your content is what truly counts."
>
> ~Gary Vaynerchuk

IMPORTANT ACTIVITIES FOR TODAY

- [ ]
- [ ]
- [ ]
- [ ]
- [ ]
- [ ]
- [ ]
- [ ]

DATE _____

SOCIAL MEDIA GOALS

WRITING GOALS

BLOGGING GOALS

IMPORTANT ACTIVITIES FOR TODAY

- [ ]
- [ ]
- [ ]
- [ ]
- [ ]
- [ ]
- [ ]
- [ ]

> "I've long advised that bloggers seeking to make money from blogging spread their interests across multiple revenue streams so as not to put all their eggs in one basket."
>
> ~Darren Rowse

DATE _____

WRITING GOALS

SOCIAL MEDIA GOALS

BLOGGING GOALS

IMPORTANT ACTIVITIES FOR TODAY

- [ ]
- [ ]
- [ ]
- [ ]
- [ ]
- [ ]
- [ ]
- [ ]

"The currency of blogging is authenticity and trust."

~Jason Calacanis

DATE _____

SOCIAL MEDIA GOALS

[Facebook]

....
....
....
....

[Twitter]

....
....
....
....

[Instagram]

....
....
....
....

[Pinterest]

....
....
....
....

WRITING GOALS

....
....
....
....
....
....
....
....
....
....
....

BLOGGING GOALS

....
....
....
....
....
....
....
....

IMPORTANT ACTIVITIES FOR TODAY

- [ ] ....
- [ ] ....
- [ ] ....
- [ ] ....
- [ ] ....
- [ ] ....
- [ ] ....
- [ ] ....

"Blogging is not a business by itself, it is only a promotional platform."

~David Risley

DATE _____

WRITING GOALS

SOCIAL MEDIA GOALS

BLOGGING GOALS

> "Successful people don't spam."
> ~Adrienne Smith

IMPORTANT ACTIVITIES FOR TODAY

- [ ]
- [ ]
- [ ]
- [ ]
- [ ]
- [ ]
- [ ]
- [ ]

DATE _____

SOCIAL MEDIA GOALS

WRITING GOALS

BLOGGING GOALS

IMPORTANT ACTIVITIES FOR TODAY

- [ ]
- [ ]
- [ ]
- [ ]
- [ ]
- [ ]
- [ ]
- [ ]

> "Blogging is good for your career. A well-executed blog sets you apart as an expert in your field."
>
> ~Penelope Trunk

DATE _____

WRITING GOALS

....
....
....
....
....
....
....
....

BLOGGING GOALS

....
....
....
....
....
....
....

SOCIAL MEDIA GOALS

f
....
....
....
....

Twitter
....
....
....

Instagram
....
....
....

Pinterest
....
....
....

> "A well-maintained blog establishes your authority in a niche by showcasing your knowledge and dedication to the topic."
>
> ~Penelope Trunk

IMPORTANT ACTIVITIES FOR TODAY

☐ ....
☐ ....
☐ ....
☐ ....
☐ ....
☐ ....
☐ ....
☐ ....
☐ ....

DATE _____

SOCIAL MEDIA GOALS

[Facebook]
....
....
....
....

[Twitter]
....
....
....
....

[Instagram]
....
....
....
....

[Pinterest]
....
....
....
....

WRITING GOALS

....
....
....
....
....
....
....
....
....
....

BLOGGING GOALS

....
....
....
....
....
....
....
....

IMPORTANT ACTIVITIES FOR TODAY

- [ ] ....
- [ ] ....
- [ ] ....
- [ ] ....
- [ ] ....
- [ ] ....
- [ ] ....
- [ ] ....

> "The internet has destroyed most of the barriers to publication. The cost of being a publisher has dropped to almost zero with two interesting immediate results: anyone can publish, and more importantly, you can publish whatever you want."
> ~Dick Costolo

DATE _____

WRITING GOALS

BLOGGING GOALS

SOCIAL MEDIA GOALS

IMPORTANT ACTIVITIES FOR TODAY

- [ ]
- [ ]
- [ ]
- [ ]
- [ ]
- [ ]
- [ ]
- [ ]

"The internet has no eraser."
~Liz Strauss

DATE _____

SOCIAL MEDIA GOALS

WRITING GOALS

BLOGGING GOALS

IMPORTANT ACTIVITIES FOR TODAY

- [ ]
- [ ]
- [ ]
- [ ]
- [ ]
- [ ]
- [ ]
- [ ]

> "In truth, the real opportunities for building authority and buzz through social meida have only just begun. You simply have to look and see where things are going instead of where they've been."
>
> ~Brian Clark

DATE _____

WRITING GOALS

....
....
....
....
....
....
....
....
....
....

SOCIAL MEDIA GOALS

[Facebook]
....
....
....
....

[Twitter]
....
....
....
....

[Instagram]
....
....
....
....

BLOGGING GOALS

....
....
....
....
....
....

[Pinterest]
....
....
....
....

> "Selling to people through social media is like going to a party, meeting somebody for the first time, and then saying, "Hey, do you want to buy this Tupperware?"
>
> ~ Pat Flynn

IMPORTANT ACTIVITIES FOR TODAY

☐ ....
☐ ....
☐ ....
☐ ....
☐ ....
☐ ....
☐ ....
☐ ....

DATE _____

SOCIAL MEDIA GOALS

[Facebook]

[Twitter]

[Instagram]

[Pinterest]

WRITING GOALS

BLOGGING GOALS

IMPORTANT ACTIVITIES FOR TODAY

- [ ]
- [ ]
- [ ]
- [ ]
- [ ]
- [ ]
- [ ]
- [ ]

> "Visual content is 40 times more likely to be shared on social media than any other type of content."

DATE _____

WRITING GOALS

....
....
....
....
....
....
....
....
....
....
....
....

BLOGGING GOALS

....
....
....
....
....
....
....

SOCIAL MEDIA GOALS

f
....
....
....
....

t
....
....
....
....

ig
....
....
....
....

p
....
....
....
....

IMPORTANT ACTIVITIES FOR TODAY

- [ ] ....
- [ ] ....
- [ ] ....
- [ ] ....
- [ ] ....
- [ ] ....
- [ ] ....
- [ ] ....

> "Social media is not a media. The key is to listen, engage, and build relationships."
>
> ~David Alston

DATE _____

SOCIAL MEDIA GOALS

f
....
....
....
....

🐦
....
....
....
....

📷
....
....
....
....

P
....
....
....
....

WRITING GOALS
....
....
....
....
....
....
....
....
....
....
....
....

BLOGGING GOALS
....
....
....
....
....
....
....
....

IMPORTANT ACTIVITIES FOR TODAY

- [ ] ....
- [ ] ....
- [ ] ....
- [ ] ....
- [ ] ....
- [ ] ....
- [ ] ....
- [ ] ....

> "Engage rather than sell ... Work as a co-creator, not a marketer."
>
> ~Tom H. C. Anderson

DATE _____

WRITING GOALS

....
....
....
....
....
....
....
....
....
....

BLOGGING GOALS

....
....
....
....
....
....
....

SOCIAL MEDIA GOALS

f
....
....
....
....

t
....
....
....
....

ig
....
....
....
....

p
....
....
....

> "Engage rather than sell ... Work as a co-creator, not a marketer."
>
> ~Tom H. C. Anderson

IMPORTANT ACTIVITIES FOR TODAY

- [ ] ....
- [ ] ....
- [ ] ....
- [ ] ....
- [ ] ....
- [ ] ....
- [ ] ....
- [ ] ....

DATE _____

SOCIAL MEDIA GOALS

f

t

ig

p

WRITING GOALS

BLOGGING GOALS

IMPORTANT ACTIVITIES FOR TODAY

- [ ]
- [ ]
- [ ]
- [ ]
- [ ]
- [ ]
- [ ]
- [ ]

> "Activate your fans, don't just collect them like baseball cards."
>
> ~Jay Baer

DATE _____

WRITING GOALS

BLOGGING GOALS

SOCIAL MEDIA GOALS

IMPORTANT ACTIVITIES FOR TODAY

- [ ]
- [ ]
- [ ]
- [ ]
- [ ]
- [ ]
- [ ]
- [ ]

> "Focus on how to be social, not on how to do social."
>
> ~Jay Baer

DATE _____

SOCIAL MEDIA GOALS

f

t

Ig

P

WRITING GOALS

BLOGGING GOALS

IMPORTANT ACTIVITIES FOR TODAY

- ☐
- ☐
- ☐
- ☐
- ☐
- ☐
- ☐
- ☐

> "If you make customers unhappy in the physical world, they might each tell 6 friends. If you make customers unhappy on the Internet, they can each tell 6,000 friends."
>
> ~Jeff Bezos

DATE _____

MONDAY	TUESDAY	WEDNESDAY
☐	☐	☐
☐	☐	☐
☐	☐	☐
☐	☐	☐
☐	☐	☐

DATE _____

THURSDAY	FRIDAY	SATURDAY / SUNDAY
☐	☐	☐
☐	☐	☐
☐	☐	☐
☐	☐	☐
☐	☐	☐

DATE _____

Newsletter Thoughts

DATE _____

Book Promotion Plans

DATE _____

WRITING GOALS

SOCIAL MEDIA GOALS

BLOGGING GOALS

IMPORTANT ACTIVITIES FOR TODAY

- [ ]
- [ ]
- [ ]
- [ ]
- [ ]
- [ ]
- [ ]
- [ ]

> "Don't say anything on-line that you wouldn't want plastered on a billboard with your face on it."
>
> ~Erin Bury

DATE _____

SOCIAL MEDIA GOALS

f
....
....
....
....

t
....
....
....
....

IG
....
....
....
....

P
....
....
....
....

WRITING GOALS

....
....
....
....
....
....
....
....
....
....
....

BLOGGING GOALS

....
....
....
....
....
....
....

IMPORTANT ACTIVITIES FOR TODAY

- [ ] ....
- [ ] ....
- [ ] ....
- [ ] ....
- [ ] ....
- [ ] ....
- [ ] ....
- [ ] ....

> "'Build it, and they will come' only works in the movies. Social Media is a 'build it, nurture it, engage them, and they may come and stay."
>
> ~Seth Godin

DATE _____

WRITING GOALS

....
....
....
....
....
....
....
....
....
....

SOCIAL MEDIA GOALS

[Facebook]
....
....
....
....

[Twitter]
....
....
....
....

[Instagram]
....
....
....
....

BLOGGING GOALS

....
....
....
....
....
....

[Pinterest]
....
....
....
....

> "Conversations among the members of your marketplace happen whether you like it or not. Good marketing encourages the right sort of conversations."
>
> ~Seth Godin

IMPORTANT ACTIVITIES FOR TODAY

- [ ] ....
- [ ] ....
- [ ] ....
- [ ] ....
- [ ] ....
- [ ] ....
- [ ] ....
- [ ] ....

DATE _____

SOCIAL MEDIA GOALS

WRITING GOALS

BLOGGING GOALS

IMPORTANT ACTIVITIES FOR TODAY

- [ ]
- [ ]
- [ ]
- [ ]
- [ ]
- [ ]
- [ ]
- [ ]

> "Social Media is about the people! Not about your business. Provide for the people and the people will provide for you."
>
> ~Matt Goulart

DATE _____

WRITING GOALS

....
....
....
....
....
....
....
....
....
....
....

BLOGGING GOALS

....
....
....
....
....
....
....

SOCIAL MEDIA GOALS

f
....
....
....
....

t
....
....
....
....

IG
....
....
....
....

P
....
....
....
....

"The value of being connected and transparent is so high that the roadbumps of privacy issues are much lower in actual experience than people's fears."

~Reid Hoffman

IMPORTANT ACTIVITIES FOR TODAY

☐ ....
☐ ....
☐ ....
☐ ....
☐ ....
☐ ....
☐ ....
☐ ....

DATE _____

SOCIAL MEDIA GOALS

[Facebook]
....
....
....
....

[Twitter]
....
....
....
....

[Instagram]
....
....
....
....

[Pinterest]
....
....
....
....

WRITING GOALS

....
....
....
....
....
....
....
....
....

BLOGGING GOALS

....
....
....
....
....
....
....

IMPORTANT ACTIVITIES FOR TODAY

- ☐ ....
- ☐ ....
- ☐ ....
- ☐ ....
- ☐ ....
- ☐ ....
- ☐ ....
- ☐ ....

> "Bring the best of your authentic self to every opportunity."
>
> ~Brian Jantsch

DATE _____

WRITING GOALS

BLOGGING GOALS

SOCIAL MEDIA GOALS

IMPORTANT ACTIVITIES FOR TODAY

- [ ]
- [ ]
- [ ]
- [ ]
- [ ]
- [ ]
- [ ]
- [ ]

> "Just be nice, take genuine interest in the people you meet, and keep in touch with people you like. This will create a group of people who are invested in helping you because they know you and appreciate you."
> ~ Guy Kawasaki

DATE _____

SOCIAL MEDIA GOALS

[f]

....
....
....
....

[twitter]

....
....
....
....

[instagram]

....
....
....
....

[pinterest]

....
....
....
....

WRITING GOALS

....
....
....
....
....
....
....
....
....
....
....
....

BLOGGING GOALS

....
....
....
....
....
....
....
....
....

IMPORTANT ACTIVITIES FOR TODAY

- ☐ ....
- ☐ ....
- ☐ ....
- ☐ ....
- ☐ ....
- ☐ ....
- ☐ ....
- ☐ ....

> "What happens in Vegas stays in Vegas; what happens on Twitter stays on Google forever!"
>
> ~Jure Klepic

DATE _____

WRITING GOALS

....
....
....
....
....
....
....
....
....
....

BLOGGING GOALS

....
....
....
....
....
....
....

SOCIAL MEDIA GOALS

f
....
....
....
....
....

t
....
....
....
....

IG
....
....
....

P
....
....
....
....

IMPORTANT ACTIVITIES FOR TODAY

☐ ....
☐ ....
☐ ....
☐ ....
☐ ....
☐ ....
☐ ....
☐ ....

> "Most bloggers who rise above the clutter are quite often prolific – they work hard, not just writing content but networking, engaging in Social Media and more."
>
> ~Darren Rowse

DATE _____

SOCIAL MEDIA GOALS

Facebook
....
....
....
....

Twitter
....
....
....
....

Instagram
....
....
....
....

Pinterest
....
....
....
....

WRITING GOALS

....
....
....
....
....
....
....
....
....
....
....

BLOGGING GOALS

....
....
....
....
....
....
....
....

IMPORTANT ACTIVITIES FOR TODAY

- [ ] ....
- [ ] ....
- [ ] ....
- [ ] ....
- [ ] ....
- [ ] ....
- [ ] ....
- [ ] ....

> "There are no magic wands, no hidden tracks, and no secret handshakes that can bring you immediate success, but with time, energy and determination you can get there."
>
> ~Darren Rowse

DATE _____

WRITING GOALS

....
....
....
....
....
....
....
....
....
....

BLOGGING GOALS

....
....
....
....
....
....
....

SOCIAL MEDIA GOALS

f
....
....
....
....

Twitter
....
....
....
....

Instagram
....
....
....
....

Pinterest
....
....
....
....

> "The qualities that make Twitter seem insane and half-baked are what makes it so powerful."
>
> ~Jonathan Zittrain

IMPORTANT ACTIVITIES FOR TODAY

- [ ] ....
- [ ] ....
- [ ] ....
- [ ] ....
- [ ] ....
- [ ] ....
- [ ] ....
- [ ] ....

DATE _____

SOCIAL MEDIA GOALS

f
....
....
....
....

t
....
....
....
....

ig
....
....
....
....

p
....
....
....
....

WRITING GOALS

....
....
....
....
....
....
....
....
....
....

BLOGGING GOALS

....
....
....
....
....
....
....

IMPORTANT ACTIVITIES FOR TODAY

- [ ] ....
- [ ] ....
- [ ] ....
- [ ] ....
- [ ] ....
- [ ] ....
- [ ] ....
- [ ] ....

> "When you give everyone a voice and give people power, the system usually ends up in a really good place."
>
> ~Mark Zuckerberg

DATE _____

WRITING GOALS

....
....
....
....
....
....
....
....
....
....
....

BLOGGING GOALS

....
....
....
....
....
....
....

SOCIAL MEDIA GOALS

f
....
....
....
....

t
....
....
....
....

ig
....
....
....
....

p
....
....
....
....

> "Never underestimate the vital importance of finding early in life the work that for you is play. This turns possible underachievers into happy warriors."
>
> ~Jeff Bullas

IMPORTANT ACTIVITIES FOR TODAY

- [ ] ....
- [ ] ....
- [ ] ....
- [ ] ....
- [ ] ....
- [ ] ....
- [ ] ....
- [ ] ....

DATE _____

SOCIAL MEDIA GOALS

WRITING GOALS

BLOGGING GOALS

IMPORTANT ACTIVITIES FOR TODAY

- [ ]
- [ ]
- [ ]
- [ ]
- [ ]
- [ ]
- [ ]
- [ ]

> "Social media is here. It's not going away; not a passing fad. Be where your customers are: in social media."
>
> ~Lori Ruff

DATE _____

WRITING GOALS

....
....
....
....
....
....
....
....
....
....

BLOGGING GOALS

....
....
....
....
....
....
....

SOCIAL MEDIA GOALS

f
....
....
....
....

t
....
....
....
....

ig
....
....
....
....

p
....
....
....

> "If you love what you do and have a sincere interest in those individuals that you meet along the journey, then not only will you benefit by your own efforts, but those you surround yourself with will be blessed with your knowledge"
> ~ Dede Watson

IMPORTANT ACTIVITIES FOR TODAY

- [ ] ....
- [ ] ....
- [ ] ....
- [ ] ....
- [ ] ....
- [ ] ....
- [ ] ....
- [ ] ....

DATE _____

SOCIAL MEDIA GOALS

[Facebook]
....
....
....
....

[Twitter]
....
....
....
....

[Instagram]
....
....
....
....

[Pinterest]
....
....
....
....

WRITING GOALS

....
....
....
....
....
....
....
....
....
....
....

BLOGGING GOALS

....
....
....
....
....
....
....

IMPORTANT ACTIVITIES FOR TODAY

☐ ....
☐ ....
☐ ....
☐ ....
☐ ....
☐ ....
☐ ....
☐ ....

> "Most of us have experienced wow moments. We just haven't taken time to think deeply about them."
>
> ~Michael Hyatt

DATE _____

WRITING GOALS

SOCIAL MEDIA GOALS

BLOGGING GOALS

IMPORTANT ACTIVITIES FOR TODAY

- [ ]
- [ ]
- [ ]
- [ ]
- [ ]
- [ ]
- [ ]
- [ ]

> "On engagement, we're already seeing that mobile users are more likely to be daily active users than desktop users. They're more likely to use Facebook six or seven days of the week."
>
> ~Mark Zuckerberg

DATE _____

SOCIAL MEDIA GOALS

f
....
....
....
....

🐦
....
....
....
....

📷
....
....
....
....

P
....
....
....
....

WRITING GOALS

....
....
....
....
....
....
....
....
....
....

BLOGGING GOALS

....
....
....
....
....
....

IMPORTANT ACTIVITIES FOR TODAY

- [ ]
- [ ]
- [ ]
- [ ]
- [ ]
- [ ]
- [ ]
- [ ]

> "Facebook is not your friend. It is a surveillance engine."
>
> ~Richard Stallman

DATE _____

WRITING GOALS

BLOGGING GOALS

SOCIAL MEDIA GOALS

f

t

ig

p

IMPORTANT ACTIVITIES FOR TODAY

- [ ]
- [ ]
- [ ]
- [ ]
- [ ]
- [ ]
- [ ]
- [ ]

> "Twitter is not a technology, it's a conversation – and it's happening with or without you."
>
> ~Charlene Li, author

DATE _____

SOCIAL MEDIA GOALS

f

t

IG

P

WRITING GOALS

BLOGGING GOALS

IMPORTANT ACTIVITIES FOR TODAY

- [ ]
- [ ]
- [ ]
- [ ]
- [ ]
- [ ]
- [ ]
- [ ]

> "When you've got 5 minutes to fill, Twitter is a great way to fill 35 minutes."
>
> ~Matt Cutts

DATE _____

WRITING GOALS

SOCIAL MEDIA GOALS

f

t

[instagram]

BLOGGING GOALS

[pinterest]

IMPORTANT ACTIVITIES FOR TODAY

- [ ]
- [ ]
- [ ]
- [ ]
- [ ]
- [ ]
- [ ]
- [ ]

"Social media is not just a spoke on the wheel of marketing. It's becoming the way entire bicycles are built."

~Ryan Lilly, author

DATE _____

SOCIAL MEDIA GOALS

f

....
....
....
....

t

....
....
....
....

ig

....
....
....
....

p

....
....
....
....

WRITING GOALS

....
....
....
....
....
....
....
....
....
....
....

BLOGGING GOALS

....
....
....
....
....
....
....

IMPORTANT ACTIVITIES FOR TODAY

- [ ] ....
- [ ] ....
- [ ] ....
- [ ] ....
- [ ] ....
- [ ] ....
- [ ] ....
- [ ] ....

> "Social media will help you build up the loyalty of your current customers to the point that they will willingly, and for free, tell others about you."
>
> ~Bonnie Sainsbury

DATE _____

WRITING GOALS

....
....
....
....
....
....
....
....
....
....
....

BLOGGING GOALS

....
....
....
....
....
....
....

SOCIAL MEDIA GOALS

f
....
....
....
....

t
....
....
....
....

i
....
....
....
....

p
....
....
....
....

"The Art of Twitter is in the Re-tweet. You Must be Interesting."
~Peter Shankman

IMPORTANT ACTIVITIES FOR TODAY

☐ ....
☐ ....
☐ ....
☐ ....
☐ ....
☐ ....
☐ ....
☐ ....

DATE _____

SOCIAL MEDIA GOALS

f
....
....
....
....

t
....
....
....
....

ig
....
....
....
....

p
....
....
....
....

WRITING GOALS

....
....
....
....
....
....
....
....
....
....
....
....

BLOGGING GOALS

....
....
....
....
....
....
....

IMPORTANT ACTIVITIES FOR TODAY

☐ ....
☐ ....
☐ ....
☐ ....
☐ ....
☐ ....
☐ ....
☐ ....

> "It's important to think of every customer as an on-line celebrity with followers, friends, & above all, influence."
>
> ~Dave Kerpen

DATE _____

WRITING GOALS

SOCIAL MEDIA GOALS

BLOGGING GOALS

IMPORTANT ACTIVITIES FOR TODAY

- [ ]
- [ ]
- [ ]
- [ ]
- [ ]
- [ ]
- [ ]
- [ ]

> "It's important to think of every customer as an online celebrity with followers, friends, & above all, influence."
>
> ~Dave Kerpen

DATE _____

SOCIAL MEDIA GOALS

[Facebook]

[Twitter]

[Instagram]

[Pinterest]

WRITING GOALS

BLOGGING GOALS

IMPORTANT ACTIVITIES FOR TODAY

- [ ]
- [ ]
- [ ]
- [ ]
- [ ]
- [ ]
- [ ]
- [ ]

> "As with any relationship, the market favors those who give more value than they ask for."
>
> ~Leslie Bradshaw

DATE _____

WRITING GOALS

....
....
....
....
....
....
....
....
....
....
....
....

BLOGGING GOALS

....
....
....
....
....
....
....

SOCIAL MEDIA GOALS

f
....
....
....
....

t
....
....
....
....

ig
....
....
....
....

p
....
....
....
....

"The ultimate content strategy is listening."
— Marcus Sheridan

IMPORTANT ACTIVITIES FOR TODAY

☐ ....
☐ ....
☐ ....
☐ ....
☐ ....
☐ ....
☐ ....
☐ ....

DATE _____

SOCIAL MEDIA GOALS

Facebook

Twitter

Instagram

Pinterest

WRITING GOALS

BLOGGING GOALS

IMPORTANT ACTIVITIES FOR TODAY

- [ ]
- [ ]
- [ ]
- [ ]
- [ ]
- [ ]
- [ ]
- [ ]

> "You're never as smart as you think you are when you are winning and never as dumb as you feel when you are losing."
>
> ~Michael Hyatt

DATE _____

WRITING GOALS

SOCIAL MEDIA GOALS

BLOGGING GOALS

IMPORTANT ACTIVITIES FOR TODAY

- [ ]
- [ ]
- [ ]
- [ ]
- [ ]
- [ ]
- [ ]
- [ ]

> "You can't take care of anyone else unless you first take care of yourself."
> ~Michael Hyatt

DATE _____

SOCIAL MEDIA GOALS

f
....
....
....
....

t
....
....
....
....

◙
....
....
....
....

P
....
....
....
....

WRITING GOALS

....
....
....
....
....
....
....
....
....

BLOGGING GOALS

....
....
....
....
....
....
....
....

IMPORTANT ACTIVITIES FOR TODAY

- [ ] ....
- [ ] ....
- [ ] ....
- [ ] ....
- [ ] ....
- [ ] ....
- [ ] ....
- [ ] ....

> "Courage is the willingness to act in spite of fear."
>
> ~Michael Hyatt

DATE _____

MONDAY	TUESDAY	WEDNESDAY
☐	☐	☐
☐	☐	☐
☐	☐	☐
☐	☐	☐
☐	☐	☐

DATE _____

THURSDAY	FRIDAY	SATURDAY / SUNDAY
☐	☐	☐
☐	☐	☐
☐	☐	☐
☐	☐	☐
☐	☐	☐

DATE _____

Newsletter Thoughts

DATE _____

Book Promotion Plans

DATE _____

WRITING GOALS

BLOGGING GOALS

SOCIAL MEDIA GOALS

IMPORTANT ACTIVITIES FOR TODAY

- [ ]
- [ ]
- [ ]
- [ ]
- [ ]
- [ ]
- [ ]
- [ ]

"Make sure your worst enemy doesn't live between your two ears."

~Laird Hamilton

DATE _____

SOCIAL MEDIA GOALS

WRITING GOALS

BLOGGING GOALS

IMPORTANT ACTIVITIES FOR TODAY

- [ ]
- [ ]
- [ ]
- [ ]
- [ ]
- [ ]
- [ ]
- [ ]

> "The greatest danger for most of us is not that we aim too high and we miss it, but we aim too low and reach it."
>
> ~ Michelangelo

DATE _____

WRITING GOALS

....
....
....
....
....
....
....
....
....
....
....
....

BLOGGING GOALS

....
....
....
....
....
....
....

SOCIAL MEDIA GOALS

f
....
....
....
....

t
....
....
....
....

ig
....
....
....
....

p
....
....
....
....

"You don't need more opportunity. You need to learn to execute on the opportunities you already have."
~Michael Hyatt

IMPORTANT ACTIVITIES FOR TODAY

☐ ....
☐ ....
☐ ....
☐ ....
☐ ....
☐ ....
☐ ....
☐ ....

DATE _____

SOCIAL MEDIA GOALS

f

t

◉

P

WRITING GOALS

BLOGGING GOALS

IMPORTANT ACTIVITIES FOR TODAY

- [ ]
- [ ]
- [ ]
- [ ]
- [ ]
- [ ]
- [ ]
- [ ]

> "You can't start the next chapter of your life if you keep re-reading the last one."
>
> ~Anonymous

DATE _____

WRITING GOALS

....
....
....
....
....
....
....
....
....
....
....
....

BLOGGING GOALS

....
....
....
....
....
....
....

SOCIAL MEDIA GOALS

f
....
....
....

t
....
....

IG
....
....
....

P
....
....
....

> "In a crowded marketplace, fitting in a failure. In a busy marketplace, not standing out is the same as being invisible."
>
> ~Seth Godin

IMPORTANT ACTIVITIES FOR TODAY

- [ ] ....
- [ ] ....
- [ ] ....
- [ ] ....
- [ ] ....
- [ ] ....
- [ ] ....
- [ ] ....

DATE _____

SOCIAL MEDIA GOALS

f
....
....
....
....

🐦
....
....
....
....

📷
....
....
....
....

P
....
....
....
....

WRITING GOALS

....
....
....
....
....
....
....
....
....
....

BLOGGING GOALS

....
....
....
....
....
....
....
....

IMPORTANT ACTIVITIES FOR TODAY

- [ ] ....
- [ ] ....
- [ ] ....
- [ ] ....
- [ ] ....
- [ ] ....
- [ ] ....
- [ ] ....

> "I learned that a long walk and calm conversation are an incredible combination if you want to build a bridge."
>
> ~Seth Godin

DATE _____

WRITING GOALS

....
....
....
....
....
....
....
....
....
....

BLOGGING GOALS

....
....
....
....
....
....
....

SOCIAL MEDIA GOALS

f
....
....
....
....

t
....
....
....
....

[instagram]
....
....
....

p
....
....
....

> "Marketing is a contest for people's attention."
>
> ~Seth Godin

IMPORTANT ACTIVITIES FOR TODAY

- [ ] ....
- [ ] ....
- [ ] ....
- [ ] ....
- [ ] ....
- [ ] ....
- [ ] ....
- [ ] ....

DATE _____

SOCIAL MEDIA GOALS

Facebook
....
....
....
....

Twitter
....
....
....
....

Instagram
....
....
....
....

Pinterest
....
....
....
....

WRITING GOALS

....
....
....
....
....
....
....
....
....
....

BLOGGING GOALS

....
....
....
....
....
....
....
....
....

IMPORTANT ACTIVITIES FOR TODAY

- [ ] ....
- [ ] ....
- [ ] ....
- [ ] ....
- [ ] ....
- [ ] ....
- [ ] ....
- [ ] ....

> "I think the most productive thing to do during times of change is to be your best self, not the best version of someone else."
>
> ~Seth Godin

DATE _____

WRITING GOALS

BLOGGING GOALS

SOCIAL MEDIA GOALS

[Facebook]

[Twitter]

[Instagram]

[Pinterest]

"Do you know what people want more than anything? They want to be missed. They want to be missed the day they don't show up. They want to be missed when they're gone."

~Seth Godin

IMPORTANT ACTIVITIES FOR TODAY

- [ ]
- [ ]
- [ ]
- [ ]
- [ ]
- [ ]
- [ ]
- [ ]

DATE _____

SOCIAL MEDIA GOALS

WRITING GOALS

BLOGGING GOALS

IMPORTANT ACTIVITIES FOR TODAY

- [ ]
- [ ]
- [ ]
- [ ]
- [ ]
- [ ]
- [ ]
- [ ]

> "One reason I encourage people to blog is that the act of doing it stretches your available vocabulary and hones a new voice."
>
> ~Seth Godin

DATE _____

WRITING GOALS

SOCIAL MEDIA GOALS

BLOGGING GOALS

"Permission marketing turns strangers into friends and friends into loyal customers. It's not just about entertainment – it's about education. Permission marketing is curriculum marketing."

~Seth Godin

IMPORTANT ACTIVITIES FOR TODAY

- [ ]
- [ ]
- [ ]
- [ ]
- [ ]
- [ ]
- [ ]
- [ ]

DATE _____

SOCIAL MEDIA GOALS

WRITING GOALS

BLOGGING GOALS

IMPORTANT ACTIVITIES FOR TODAY

- [ ]
- [ ]
- [ ]
- [ ]
- [ ]
- [ ]
- [ ]
- [ ]

> "I made a decision to write for my readers, not to try to find more readers for my writing."
>
> ~Seth Godin

DATE _____

WRITING GOALS

SOCIAL MEDIA GOALS

BLOGGING GOALS

IMPORTANT ACTIVITIES FOR TODAY

- [ ]
- [ ]
- [ ]
- [ ]
- [ ]
- [ ]
- [ ]
- [ ]

> "Stop getting distracted by things that have nothing to do with your dreams."

DATE _____

SOCIAL MEDIA GOALS

WRITING GOALS

BLOGGING GOALS

IMPORTANT ACTIVITIES FOR TODAY

- [ ]
- [ ]
- [ ]
- [ ]
- [ ]
- [ ]
- [ ]
- [ ]

> "Stop telling yourself you don't know what to do. Yes, you do. Listen to your intuition and trust yourself."
>
> ~Katherine Sullivan

DATE _____

WRITING GOALS

....
....
....
....
....
....
....
....
....
....
....

BLOGGING GOALS

....
....
....
....
....
....
....

SOCIAL MEDIA GOALS

f
....
....
....
....

t
....
....
....
....

IG
....
....
....
....

P
....
....
....

"Don't ask people for directions when they've never been where you are going."
~Katherine Sullivan

IMPORTANT ACTIVITIES FOR TODAY

☐ ....
☐ ....
☐ ....
☐ ....
☐ ....
☐ ....
☐ ....
☐ ....
☐ ....

DATE _____

SOCIAL MEDIA GOALS

[f]

[twitter]

[instagram]

[pinterest]

WRITING GOALS

BLOGGING GOALS

IMPORTANT ACTIVITIES FOR TODAY

- [ ]
- [ ]
- [ ]
- [ ]
- [ ]
- [ ]
- [ ]
- [ ]

> "Don't use social media to impress people; use it to impact people."
>
> ~Dave Willis

DATE _____

WRITING GOALS

SOCIAL MEDIA GOALS

BLOGGING GOALS

IMPORTANT ACTIVITIES FOR TODAY

- [ ]
- [ ]
- [ ]
- [ ]
- [ ]
- [ ]
- [ ]
- [ ]

"Be Authentic."

DATE _____

SOCIAL MEDIA GOALS

WRITING GOALS

BLOGGING GOALS

IMPORTANT ACTIVITIES FOR TODAY

- [ ]
- [ ]
- [ ]
- [ ]
- [ ]
- [ ]
- [ ]
- [ ]

"A goal should scare you a little, & excite you A LOT."

~Joe Vitale

DATE _____

WRITING GOALS

SOCIAL MEDIA GOALS

BLOGGING GOALS

"Surround yourself with those on the same mission as you."

IMPORTANT ACTIVITIES FOR TODAY

- [ ]
- [ ]
- [ ]
- [ ]
- [ ]
- [ ]
- [ ]
- [ ]

DATE _____

SOCIAL MEDIA GOALS

f
....
....
....
....

t
....
....
....
....

IG
....
....
....
....

P
....
....
....
....

WRITING GOALS

....
....
....
....
....
....
....
....
....
....
....
....

BLOGGING GOALS

....
....
....
....
....
....
....
....

IMPORTANT ACTIVITIES FOR TODAY

- [ ] ....
- [ ] ....
- [ ] ....
- [ ] ....
- [ ] ....
- [ ] ....
- [ ] ....
- [ ] ....

> "It's your road, and yours alone. Others may walk it with you, but no one can walk it for you."
>
> ~ Rumi

DATE _____

WRITING GOALS

SOCIAL MEDIA GOALS

BLOGGING GOALS

IMPORTANT ACTIVITIES FOR TODAY

- [ ]
- [ ]
- [ ]
- [ ]
- [ ]
- [ ]
- [ ]
- [ ]

"Never think that what you have to offer is insignificant. There will always be someone out there that needs what you have to give."

DATE _____

SOCIAL MEDIA GOALS

WRITING GOALS

BLOGGING GOALS

IMPORTANT ACTIVITIES FOR TODAY

- [ ]
- [ ]
- [ ]
- [ ]
- [ ]
- [ ]
- [ ]
- [ ]

> "Without strategy, content is just stuff, and the world has enough stuff."
>
> ~ @arjunbasu

DATE _____

WRITING GOALS

BLOGGING GOALS

SOCIAL MEDIA GOALS

Facebook

Twitter

Instagram

Pinterest

> "Marketing is enthusiasm transferred to the customer."
> ~Gregory Ciotti

IMPORTANT ACTIVITIES FOR TODAY

- [ ]
- [ ]
- [ ]
- [ ]
- [ ]
- [ ]
- [ ]
- [ ]

DATE _____

SOCIAL MEDIA GOALS

f
....
....
....
....

t
....
....
....
....

[o]
....
....
....
....

p
....
....
....
....

WRITING GOALS

....
....
....
....
....
....
....
....
....
....

BLOGGING GOALS

....
....
....
....
....
....
....

IMPORTANT ACTIVITIES FOR TODAY

- [ ] ....
- [ ] ....
- [ ] ....
- [ ] ....
- [ ] ....
- [ ] ....
- [ ] ....
- [ ] ....

> "People do not buy goods and services. They buy relations, stories and magic."
>
> ~Seth Godin

DATE _____

WRITING GOALS

BLOGGING GOALS

SOCIAL MEDIA GOALS

IMPORTANT ACTIVITIES FOR TODAY

- [ ]
- [ ]
- [ ]
- [ ]
- [ ]
- [ ]
- [ ]
- [ ]

"Stop selling, start helping."

~Zig Zigler

DATE _____

SOCIAL MEDIA GOALS

WRITING GOALS

BLOGGING GOALS

IMPORTANT ACTIVITIES FOR TODAY

- [ ]
- [ ]
- [ ]
- [ ]
- [ ]
- [ ]
- [ ]
- [ ]

"Marketing is no longer about the stuff yo make, but about the stories you tell."

~Seth Godin

DATE _____

WRITING GOALS

SOCIAL MEDIA GOALS

BLOGGING GOALS

"Don't deliver a Product – Deliver an Experience"

IMPORTANT ACTIVITIES FOR TODAY

- [ ]
- [ ]
- [ ]
- [ ]
- [ ]
- [ ]
- [ ]
- [ ]
- [ ]

DATE _____

SOCIAL MEDIA GOALS

f

t

I

P

WRITING GOALS

BLOGGING GOALS

IMPORTANT ACTIVITIES FOR TODAY

- [ ]
- [ ]
- [ ]
- [ ]
- [ ]
- [ ]
- [ ]
- [ ]

> "Strive not to be a success, but rather to be of value."
>
> ~Albert Einstein

DATE _____

WRITING GOALS

BLOGGING GOALS

SOCIAL MEDIA GOALS

IMPORTANT ACTIVITIES FOR TODAY

"Be a resource, not a sales pitch."

DATE _____

SOCIAL MEDIA GOALS

f
....
....
....
....

t
....
....
....
....

📷
....
....
....
....

P
....
....
....
....

WRITING GOALS

....
....
....
....
....
....
....
....
....
....

BLOGGING GOALS

....
....
....
....
....
....
....

IMPORTANT ACTIVITIES FOR TODAY

- [ ] ....
- [ ] ....
- [ ] ....
- [ ] ....
- [ ] ....
- [ ] ....
- [ ] ....
- [ ] ....

> "The best marketing strategy ever: CARE."
>
> ~Gary Vaynerchuk

DATE _____

MONDAY	TUESDAY	WEDNESDAY
☐	☐	☐
☐	☐	☐
☐	☐	☐
☐	☐	☐
☐	☐	☐

DATE _____

THURSDAY	FRIDAY	SATURDAY / SUNDAY
☐	☐	☐
☐	☐	☐
☐	☐	☐
☐	☐	☐
☐	☐	☐

DATE _____

Newsletter Thoughts

DATE _____

Book Promotion Plans

DATE _____

WRITING GOALS

SOCIAL MEDIA GOALS

BLOGGING GOALS

"Branding is what people say about you when you are not in the room."

IMPORTANT ACTIVITIES FOR TODAY

- [ ]
- [ ]
- [ ]
- [ ]
- [ ]
- [ ]
- [ ]
- [ ]
- [ ]

DATE _____

SOCIAL MEDIA GOALS

Facebook

Twitter

Instagram

Pinterest

WRITING GOALS

BLOGGING GOALS

IMPORTANT ACTIVITIES FOR TODAY

- [ ]
- [ ]
- [ ]
- [ ]
- [ ]
- [ ]
- [ ]
- [ ]

> "Marketing without data is like driving with your eyes closed."
>
> ~Dan Zarella

DATE _____

WRITING GOALS

....
....
....
....
....
....
....
....
....
....
....

BLOGGING GOALS

....
....
....
....
....
....
....

SOCIAL MEDIA GOALS

f

....
....
....
....

t

....
....
....
....

ig

....
....
....

p

....
....
....

> "Everyone is not your customer."
> ~Seth Godin

IMPORTANT ACTIVITIES FOR TODAY

☐ ....
☐ ....
☐ ....
☐ ....
☐ ....
☐ ....
☐ ....
☐ ....

DATE _____

SOCIAL MEDIA GOALS

WRITING GOALS

BLOGGING GOALS

IMPORTANT ACTIVITIES FOR TODAY

- [ ]
- [ ]
- [ ]
- [ ]
- [ ]
- [ ]
- [ ]
- [ ]

> "To give real service, you must add something which cannot be bought or measured with money, and that is sincerity and integrity."
>
> ~Douglas Adams

DATE _____

WRITING GOALS

SOCIAL MEDIA GOALS

BLOGGING GOALS

IMPORTANT ACTIVITIES FOR TODAY

- [ ]
- [ ]
- [ ]
- [ ]
- [ ]
- [ ]
- [ ]
- [ ]

> "Content is fire, Social Media is gasoline."
> ~Jay Baer

DATE _____

SOCIAL MEDIA GOALS

WRITING GOALS

BLOGGING GOALS

IMPORTANT ACTIVITIES FOR TODAY

- [ ]
- [ ]
- [ ]
- [ ]
- [ ]
- [ ]
- [ ]
- [ ]

> "The best advertising you can have is a loyal customer spreading the word about how incredible your business is."
>
> ~Shep Hyken

DATE _____

WRITING GOALS

SOCIAL MEDIA GOALS

BLOGGING GOALS

"Supporting another's success won't ever dampen yours."

IMPORTANT ACTIVITIES FOR TODAY

- [ ]
- [ ]
- [ ]
- [ ]
- [ ]
- [ ]
- [ ]
- [ ]

DATE _____

SOCIAL MEDIA GOALS

f
....
....
....
....

t
....
....
....
....

[IG]
....
....
....
....

P
....
....
....
....

WRITING GOALS

....
....
....
....
....
....
....
....
....
....

BLOGGING GOALS

....
....
....
....
....
....
....
....
....

IMPORTANT ACTIVITIES FOR TODAY

- ☐ ....
- ☐ ....
- ☐ ....
- ☐ ....
- ☐ ....
- ☐ ....
- ☐ ....
- ☐ ....

> "Maybe don't call it social media. Just be human and tell your story."
>
> ~ Gary Vaynerchuck

DATE _____

WRITING GOALS

....
....
....
....
....
....
....
....
....
....

BLOGGING GOALS

....
....
....
....
....
....
....

SOCIAL MEDIA GOALS

f
....
....
....
....

t
....
....
....
....

ig
....
....
....

p
....
....
....

> "Google only loves you when everyone else loves you first."
> ~Wendy Piersall

IMPORTANT ACTIVITIES FOR TODAY

- [ ] ....
- [ ] ....
- [ ] ....
- [ ] ....
- [ ] ....
- [ ] ....
- [ ] ....
- [ ] ....

DATE _____

SOCIAL MEDIA GOALS

f
....
....
....
....

Twitter
....
....
....
....

Instagram
....
....
....
....

Pinterest
....
....
....
....

WRITING GOALS

....
....
....
....
....
....
....
....
....
....

BLOGGING GOALS

....
....
....
....
....
....
....

IMPORTANT ACTIVITIES FOR TODAY

- [ ] ....
- [ ] ....
- [ ] ....
- [ ] ....
- [ ] ....
- [ ] ....
- [ ] ....
- [ ] ....

"Consumers do not buy products. They buy product benefits."

~David Ogilvy

DATE _____

WRITING GOALS

SOCIAL MEDIA GOALS

BLOGGING GOALS

IMPORTANT ACTIVITIES FOR TODAY

- [ ]
- [ ]
- [ ]
- [ ]
- [ ]
- [ ]
- [ ]
- [ ]

"Leadership is the ability to hide your panic from others."
~Lao Tuz

DATE _____

SOCIAL MEDIA GOALS

f
....
....
....
....

t
....
....
....
....

ig
....
....
....
....

p
....
....
....
....

WRITING GOALS

....
....
....
....
....
....
....
....
....
....

BLOGGING GOALS

....
....
....
....
....
....

IMPORTANT ACTIVITIES FOR TODAY

- [ ] ....
- [ ] ....
- [ ] ....
- [ ] ....
- [ ] ....
- [ ] ....
- [ ] ....
- [ ] ....

> "You have to learn the rules of the game and then you have to play better than anyone else."
>
> ~Albert Einstein

DATE _____

WRITING GOALS

SOCIAL MEDIA GOALS

BLOGGING GOALS

IMPORTANT ACTIVITIES FOR TODAY

- [ ]
- [ ]
- [ ]
- [ ]
- [ ]
- [ ]
- [ ]
- [ ]

"If you want something you never had, you need to do something you've never done."

DATE _____

SOCIAL MEDIA GOALS

[Facebook]

....
....
....
....

[Twitter]

....
....
....
....

[Instagram]

....
....
....
....

[Pinterest]

....
....
....
....

WRITING GOALS

....
....
....
....
....
....
....
....
....

BLOGGING GOALS

....
....
....
....
....
....

IMPORTANT ACTIVITIES FOR TODAY

- [ ] ....
- [ ] ....
- [ ] ....
- [ ] ....
- [ ] ....
- [ ] ....
- [ ] ....
- [ ] ....

> "Sell the problem you solve, not the product."
> ~Zac Efron

DATE _____

WRITING GOALS

SOCIAL MEDIA GOALS

BLOGGING GOALS

"If someone offers you an amazing opportunity and you're not sure you can do it, say yes – then learn how to do it later."

~Richard Branson

IMPORTANT ACTIVITIES FOR TODAY

- [ ]
- [ ]
- [ ]
- [ ]
- [ ]
- [ ]
- [ ]
- [ ]

DATE _____

SOCIAL MEDIA GOALS

f
....
....
....
....

t
....
....
....
....

IG
....
....
....
....

P
....
....
....
....

WRITING GOALS

....
....
....
....
....
....
....
....
....
....

BLOGGING GOALS

....
....
....
....
....
....
....
....

IMPORTANT ACTIVITIES FOR TODAY

☐ ....
☐ ....
☐ ....
☐ ....
☐ ....
☐ ....
☐ ....
☐ ....

> "The best marketing doesn't feel like marketing"
>
> ~Tom Fishbourne

DATE _____

WRITING GOALS

....
....
....
....
....
....
....
....
....
....
....

BLOGGING GOALS

....
....
....
....
....
....
....
....

SOCIAL MEDIA GOALS

f
....
....
....
....

t
....
....
....
....

IG
....
....
....

P
....
....
....

"Advertising is saying you're good. PR is getting someone else to say you're good."

~Jean-Louis Gassee

IMPORTANT ACTIVITIES FOR TODAY

- [ ] ....
- [ ] ....
- [ ] ....
- [ ] ....
- [ ] ....
- [ ] ....
- [ ] ....
- [ ] ....
- [ ] ....

DATE _____

SOCIAL MEDIA GOALS

f
....
....
....
....

t
....
....
....
....

ig
....
....
....
....

p
....
....
....
....

WRITING GOALS

....
....
....
....
....
....
....
....
....

BLOGGING GOALS

....
....
....
....
....
....

IMPORTANT ACTIVITIES FOR TODAY

- [ ]
- [ ] ....
- [ ] ....
- [ ] ....
- [ ] ....
- [ ] ....
- [ ] ....
- [ ] ....

> "Either write something worth reading or do something worth writing."
>
> ~Benjamin Franklin

DATE _____

WRITING GOALS

BLOGGING GOALS

SOCIAL MEDIA GOALS

[Facebook]

[Twitter]

[Instagram]

[Pinterest]

IMPORTANT ACTIVITIES FOR TODAY

- [ ]
- [ ]
- [ ]
- [ ]
- [ ]
- [ ]
- [ ]
- [ ]

> "If you don't track your visits and visitors on your website then how can you tell if your social media presence is actually making a difference?"
>
> ~Ian Anderson Gray

DATE _____

SOCIAL MEDIA GOALS

f
....
....
....
....

🐦
....
....
....
....

📷
....
....
....
....

P
....
....
....
....

WRITING GOALS
....
....
....
....
....
....
....
....
....
....
....

BLOGGING GOALS
....
....
....
....
....
....
....

IMPORTANT ACTIVITIES FOR TODAY

- [ ] ....
- [ ] ....
- [ ] ....
- [ ] ....
- [ ] ....
- [ ] ....
- [ ] ....
- [ ] ....

> "The goal of social media is to turn customers into a volunteer marketing army."
>
> ~Jay Baer

DATE _____

WRITING GOALS

....
....
....
....
....
....
....
....
....
....

BLOGGING GOALS

....
....
....
....
....
....
....

SOCIAL MEDIA GOALS

f
....
....
....
....

t
....
....
....
....

ig
....
....
....
....

p
....
....
....
....

> "When you say it – it's marketing. When they say it – its social proof."
> ~Andy Crestodina

IMPORTANT ACTIVITIES FOR TODAY

- [ ] ....
- [ ] ....
- [ ] ....
- [ ] ....
- [ ] ....
- [ ] ....
- [ ] ....
- [ ] ....
- [ ] ....

DATE _____

SOCIAL MEDIA GOALS

WRITING GOALS

BLOGGING GOALS

IMPORTANT ACTIVITIES FOR TODAY

- [ ]
- [ ]
- [ ]
- [ ]
- [ ]
- [ ]
- [ ]
- [ ]

"The best content spreads by itself."

~Brian Clark

DATE _____

WRITING GOALS

SOCIAL MEDIA GOALS

f

t

◉

p

BLOGGING GOALS

IMPORTANT ACTIVITIES FOR TODAY

- [ ]
- [ ]
- [ ]
- [ ]
- [ ]
- [ ]
- [ ]
- [ ]
- [ ]

> "Kids are using social media the RIGHT way. They are using it to communicate."
>
> ~Ted Rubin

DATE _____

SOCIAL MEDIA GOALS

WRITING GOALS

BLOGGING GOALS

IMPORTANT ACTIVITIES FOR TODAY

- [ ]
- [ ]
- [ ]
- [ ]
- [ ]
- [ ]
- [ ]
- [ ]

> "If what you are saying doesn't add value they won't listen to you."
>
> ~Marcus Sheridan

DATE _____

WRITING GOALS

....
....
....
....
....
....
....
....
....
....

BLOGGING GOALS

....
....
....
....
....
....
....

SOCIAL MEDIA GOALS

f
....
....
....
....

Twitter
....
....
....
....

Instagram
....
....
....
....

Pinterest
....
....
....
....

> "Never build your content ship on rented land."
>
> ~Joe Pulizzi

IMPORTANT ACTIVITIES FOR TODAY

- [ ] ....
- [ ] ....
- [ ] ....
- [ ] ....
- [ ] ....
- [ ] ....
- [ ] ....
- [ ] ....

DATE _____

SOCIAL MEDIA GOALS

f
....
....
....
....

t
....
....
....
....

ig
....
....
....
....

p
....
....
....
....

WRITING GOALS

....
....
....
....
....
....
....
....
....
....

BLOGGING GOALS

....
....
....
....
....
....
....

IMPORTANT ACTIVITIES FOR TODAY

- [ ] ....
- [ ] ....
- [ ] ....
- [ ] ....
- [ ] ....
- [ ] ....
- [ ] ....
- [ ] ....

> "Content that helps is superior to content that sells."
>
> ~Jay Baer

DATE _____

WRITING GOALS

BLOGGING GOALS

SOCIAL MEDIA GOALS

IMPORTANT ACTIVITIES FOR TODAY

- [ ]
- [ ]
- [ ]
- [ ]
- [ ]
- [ ]
- [ ]
- [ ]

> "We are in the business of listening, communicating, teaching and helping."
>
> ~Marcus Sheridan

DATE _____

SOCIAL MEDIA GOALS

WRITING GOALS

BLOGGING GOALS

IMPORTANT ACTIVITIES FOR TODAY

- [ ]
- [ ]
- [ ]
- [ ]
- [ ]
- [ ]
- [ ]
- [ ]
- [ ]

> "Power doesn't come from CONTENT, power comes from content that MOVES.
>
> ~Mark Schaefer

DATE _____

WRITING GOALS

BLOGGING GOALS

SOCIAL MEDIA GOALS

IMPORTANT ACTIVITIES FOR TODAY

- [ ]
- [ ]
- [ ]
- [ ]
- [ ]
- [ ]
- [ ]
- [ ]

> "Find your sweet spot: the intersection between what you know & what your customers need to know."
>
> ~Joe Pulizzi

DATE _____

SOCIAL MEDIA GOALS

[Facebook]
....
....
....
....

[Twitter]
....
....
....
....

[Instagram]
....
....
....
....

[Pinterest]
....
....
....
....

WRITING GOALS

....
....
....
....
....
....
....
....
....
....
....
....

BLOGGING GOALS

....
....
....
....
....
....
....

IMPORTANT ACTIVITIES FOR TODAY

☐ ....
☐ ....
☐ ....
☐ ....
☐ ....
☐ ....
☐ ....
☐ ....

> "Ask what you can do for influencers, not what influencers can do for you – develop relationships!
>
> ~Laura Fitton

DATE _____

MONDAY	TUESDAY	WEDNESDAY
☐	☐	☐
☐	☐	☐
☐	☐	☐
☐	☐	☐
☐	☐	☐

DATE _____

THURSDAY	FRIDAY	SATURDAY / SUNDAY
☐	☐	☐
☐	☐	☐
☐	☐	☐
☐	☐	☐
☐	☐	☐

DATE _____

Newsletter Thoughts

DATE _____

Book Promotion Plans

DATE _____

WRITING GOALS

BLOGGING GOALS

SOCIAL MEDIA GOALS

IMPORTANT ACTIVITIES FOR TODAY

- [ ]
- [ ]
- [ ]
- [ ]
- [ ]
- [ ]
- [ ]
- [ ]

"When you connect with influencers and use their content, you build your own influence as well."

~Lee Odden

DATE _____

SOCIAL MEDIA GOALS

f

🐦

📷

P

WRITING GOALS

BLOGGING GOALS

IMPORTANT ACTIVITIES FOR TODAY

- ☐
- ☐
- ☐
- ☐
- ☐
- ☐
- ☐
- ☐

> "Lead with a personal story. Give your audience a way to connect and show you're a real person.
>
> ~Michael Hyatt

DATE _____

WRITING GOALS

SOCIAL MEDIA GOALS

f

t

○

BLOGGING GOALS

P

> "Relationships are like muscle tissue, the more they are engaged, the stronger and more valuable they become."
>
> ~Ted Rubin

IMPORTANT ACTIVITIES FOR TODAY

- [ ]
- [ ]
- [ ]
- [ ]
- [ ]
- [ ]
- [ ]
- [ ]

DATE _____

SOCIAL MEDIA GOALS

f

t

IG

P

WRITING GOALS

BLOGGING GOALS

IMPORTANT ACTIVITIES FOR TODAY

- [ ]
- [ ]
- [ ]
- [ ]
- [ ]
- [ ]
- [ ]
- [ ]

"Whoever generates the most trust on-line wins."

~Marcus Sherida

DATE _____

WRITING GOALS

SOCIAL MEDIA GOALS

BLOGGING GOALS

IMPORTANT ACTIVITIES FOR TODAY

- [ ]
- [ ]
- [ ]
- [ ]
- [ ]
- [ ]
- [ ]
- [ ]

> "When finished writing a post, go back & add bullets, sub heads, spacing; eliminate long paragraphs or sentences."
>
> ~Michael Hyatt

DATE _____

SOCIAL MEDIA GOALS

f
....
....
....
....

t
....
....
....
....

○
....
....
....
....

p
....
....
....
....

WRITING GOALS

....
....
....
....
....
....
....
....
....
....
....
....

BLOGGING GOALS

....
....
....
....
....
....
....
....

IMPORTANT ACTIVITIES FOR TODAY

☐ ....
☐ ....
☐ ....
☐ ....
☐ ....
☐ ....
☐ ....
☐ ....

> "Social media is not an end in itself. It's just another tool to reach people."
>
> ~Simon Mainwaring

DATE _____

WRITING GOALS

....
....
....
....
....
....
....
....
....
....
....
....

BLOGGING GOALS

....
....
....
....
....
....
....

SOCIAL MEDIA GOALS

f
....
....
....
....

t
....
....
....
....

IG
....
....
....

P
....
....
....

> "Social media policies will never be able to cure stupid."
> ~Nichole Kelly

IMPORTANT ACTIVITIES FOR TODAY

- [ ] ....
- [ ] ....
- [ ] ....
- [ ] ....
- [ ] ....
- [ ] ....
- [ ] ....
- [ ] ....

DATE _____

SOCIAL MEDIA GOALS

f
....
....
....
....

t
....
....
....
....

◉
....
....
....
....

p
....
....
....
....

WRITING GOALS

....
....
....
....
....
....
....
....
....
....
....

BLOGGING GOALS

....
....
....
....
....
....
....
....

IMPORTANT ACTIVITIES FOR TODAY

☐ ....
☐ ....
☐ ....
☐ ....
☐ ....
☐ ....
☐ ....
☐ ....

> "Saying hello doesn't have an ROI. It's about building relationships."
>
> ~Gary Vaynerchuk

DATE _____

WRITING GOALS

BLOGGING GOALS

SOCIAL MEDIA GOALS

IMPORTANT ACTIVITIES FOR TODAY

> "Be selective. Just because a particular social media channel exists doesn't mean it's right for your business."
>
> ~markarmstrongillustrations.com

DATE _____

SOCIAL MEDIA GOALS

WRITING GOALS

BLOGGING GOALS

IMPORTANT ACTIVITIES FOR TODAY

- [ ]
- [ ]
- [ ]
- [ ]
- [ ]
- [ ]
- [ ]
- [ ]

> "Social media creates communities, not markets."
>
> ~Don Schultz

DATE _____

WRITING GOALS

....
....
....
....
....
....
....
....
....

BLOGGING GOALS

....
....
....
....
....
....
....

SOCIAL MEDIA GOALS

f
....
....
....
....

t
....
....
....
....

[ig]
....
....

p
....
....
....

> "Only one mode of communication with your ideal prospects remains steadfast in the face of a changing social media landscape – Email."
>
> ~Amy Porterfield

IMPORTANT ACTIVITIES FOR TODAY

- [ ] ....
- [ ] ....
- [ ] ....
- [ ] ....
- [ ] ....
- [ ] ....
- [ ] ....
- [ ] ....

DATE _____

SOCIAL MEDIA GOALS

f

t

ig

p

WRITING GOALS

BLOGGING GOALS

IMPORTANT ACTIVITIES FOR TODAY

- [ ]
- [ ]
- [ ]
- [ ]
- [ ]
- [ ]
- [ ]
- [ ]

> "Learn from those that are getting results and model what's already working."
>
> ~Amy Porterfield

DATE _____

WRITING GOALS

BLOGGING GOALS

SOCIAL MEDIA GOALS

f

t

ig

p

IMPORTANT ACTIVITIES FOR TODAY

- [ ]
- [ ]
- [ ]
- [ ]
- [ ]
- [ ]
- [ ]
- [ ]
- [ ]

"Take Action daily to move your business forward."

~Amy Porterfield

DATE _____

SOCIAL MEDIA GOALS

Facebook

Twitter

Instagram

Pinterest

WRITING GOALS

BLOGGING GOALS

IMPORTANT ACTIVITIES FOR TODAY

- [ ]
- [ ]
- [ ]
- [ ]
- [ ]
- [ ]
- [ ]
- [ ]

> "I like to say that Twitter is like a bar, Facebook is your living room and LinkedIn is the local chamber of commerce."
>
> ~BSStoltz

DATE _____

WRITING GOALS

SOCIAL MEDIA GOALS

BLOGGING GOALS

IMPORTANT ACTIVITIES FOR TODAY

- [ ]
- [ ]
- [ ]
- [ ]
- [ ]
- [ ]
- [ ]
- [ ]

> "There are THREE sides to every online interaction: Yours, mine and the view of everyone watching us. Act carefully."
>
> ~Mack Collier

DATE _____

SOCIAL MEDIA GOALS

f
....
....
....
....

Twitter
....
....
....
....

Instagram
....
....
....
....

Pinterest
....
....
....
....

WRITING GOALS

....
....
....
....
....
....
....
....
....
....
....
....

BLOGGING GOALS

....
....
....
....
....
....
....

IMPORTANT ACTIVITIES FOR TODAY

- [ ] ....
- [ ] ....
- [ ] ....
- [ ] ....
- [ ] ....
- [ ] ....
- [ ] ....
- [ ] ....

> "Social media is a lot like the dating process. I want flowers and chocolates and all the fun repartee that goes along with a new relationship."
>
> ~Rebekah Radice

DATE _____

WRITING GOALS

SOCIAL MEDIA GOALS

f

t

IG

P

BLOGGING GOALS

IMPORTANT ACTIVITIES FOR TODAY

- [ ]
- [ ]
- [ ]
- [ ]
- [ ]
- [ ]
- [ ]
- [ ]

"No matter what people tell you, words and ideas can change the world."

~ Robin Williams

DATE _____

SOCIAL MEDIA GOALS

WRITING GOALS

BLOGGING GOALS

IMPORTANT ACTIVITIES FOR TODAY

- [ ]
- [ ]
- [ ]
- [ ]
- [ ]
- [ ]
- [ ]
- [ ]

> "Social tools are not just about giving people a voice, but giving them a way to collaborate, contribute and connect."
>
> ~John Stepper

DATE _____

WRITING GOALS

SOCIAL MEDIA GOALS

BLOGGING GOALS

IMPORTANT ACTIVITIES FOR TODAY

- [ ]
- [ ]
- [ ]
- [ ]
- [ ]
- [ ]
- [ ]
- [ ]

> "Don't focus on having a great blog. Focus on producing a blog that's good for your readers."
>
> ~Brian Clark

DATE _____

SOCIAL MEDIA GOALS

WRITING GOALS

BLOGGING GOALS

IMPORTANT ACTIVITIES FOR TODAY

- [ ]
- [ ]
- [ ]
- [ ]
- [ ]
- [ ]
- [ ]
- [ ]

> "As a blogger, everything that you do flows from understanding your audience and seeking to help them as much as possible."
>
> ~Brian Clark

DATE _____

WRITING GOALS

SOCIAL MEDIA GOALS

BLOGGING GOALS

"Blogging is a conversation, not a quote."
~Mike Butcher

IMPORTANT ACTIVITIES FOR TODAY

☐
☐
☐
☐
☐
☐
☐
☐

DATE _____

SOCIAL MEDIA GOALS

WRITING GOALS

BLOGGING GOALS

IMPORTANT ACTIVITIES FOR TODAY

- [ ]
- [ ]
- [ ]
- [ ]
- [ ]
- [ ]
- [ ]
- [ ]

> "Blogging is only as interesting as the interest shown in others."
>
> ~Lee Odden

DATE _____

WRITING GOALS

SOCIAL MEDIA GOALS

BLOGGING GOALS

IMPORTANT ACTIVITIES FOR TODAY

- [ ]
- [ ]
- [ ]
- [ ]
- [ ]
- [ ]
- [ ]
- [ ]

> "Blogging is just writing – writing using a particularly efficient type of publishing technology."
>
> ~Simon Dumenco

DATE _____

SOCIAL MEDIA GOALS

f
....
....
....
....

t
....
....
....
....

IG
....
....
....
....

P
....
....
....
....

WRITING GOALS
....
....
....
....
....
....
....
....
....
....

BLOGGING GOALS
....
....
....
....
....
....
....

IMPORTANT ACTIVITIES FOR TODAY

- [ ] ....
- [ ] ....
- [ ] ....
- [ ] ....
- [ ] ....
- [ ] ....
- [ ] ....
- [ ] ....

> "Blogging is to writing what extreme sports are to athletics: more free-form, more accident-prone, less formal, more alive. It is, in many ways, writing out loud."
>
> ~Andrew Sullivan

DATE _____

WRITING GOALS

....
....
....
....
....
....
....
....
....
....
....
....
....

BLOGGING GOALS

....
....
....
....
....
....
....

SOCIAL MEDIA GOALS

f
....
....
....

t
....
....
....

IG
....
....
....

P
....
....
....

> "Blogging is a communication mechanism handed to us by the long tail of the internet."
> ~Tom Foremski

IMPORTANT ACTIVITIES FOR TODAY

- [ ] ....
- [ ] ....
- [ ] ....
- [ ] ....
- [ ] ....
- [ ] ....
- [ ] ....
- [ ] ....

DATE _____

SOCIAL MEDIA GOALS

WRITING GOALS

BLOGGING GOALS

IMPORTANT ACTIVITIES FOR TODAY

- [ ]
- [ ]
- [ ]
- [ ]
- [ ]
- [ ]
- [ ]
- [ ]

> "The first thing you need to decide when you build your blog is what you want to accomplish with it, and what it can do if successful."
>
> ~Ron Dawson

DATE _____

WRITING GOALS

....
....
....
....
....
....
....
....
....
....

SOCIAL MEDIA GOALS

f

....
....
....
....

t

....
....
....

◙

....
....
....

BLOGGING GOALS

....
....
....
....
....
....

P

....
....
....

> "Don't try to plan everything out to the very last detail. I'm a big believer in just getting it out there: Create a minimal viable product or website, launch it, and get feedback."
>
> ~Neil Patel

IMPORTANT ACTIVITIES FOR TODAY

☐ ....
☐ ....
☐ ....
☐ ....
☐ ....
☐ ....
☐ ....
☐ ....

DATE _____

SOCIAL MEDIA GOALS

WRITING GOALS

BLOGGING GOALS

IMPORTANT ACTIVITIES FOR TODAY

- [ ]
- [ ]
- [ ]
- [ ]
- [ ]
- [ ]
- [ ]
- [ ]

"The casual conversational tone of a blog is what makes it particularly dangerous."

~Daniel B. Beaulieu

DATE _____

WRITING GOALS

SOCIAL MEDIA GOALS

f

t

ig

p

BLOGGING GOALS

> "Not only are bloggers suckers for the remarkable, so are the people who read blogs."
>
> ~Seth Godin

IMPORTANT ACTIVITIES FOR TODAY

- [ ]
- [ ]
- [ ]
- [ ]
- [ ]
- [ ]
- [ ]
- [ ]

DATE _____

SOCIAL MEDIA GOALS

f
....
....
....
....

t
....
....
....
....

IG
....
....
....
....

P
....
....
....
....

WRITING GOALS

....
....
....
....
....
....
....
....
....
....
....

BLOGGING GOALS

....
....
....
....
....
....
....
....

IMPORTANT ACTIVITIES FOR TODAY

- [ ] ....
- [ ] ....
- [ ] ....
- [ ] ....
- [ ] ....
- [ ] ....
- [ ] ....
- [ ] ....

> "When you write remarkable content, you stay engaged and excited with your blog. Your readers follow suit."
>
> ~Seth Godin

DATE _____

MONDAY	TUESDAY	WEDNESDAY
☐	☐	☐
☐	☐	☐
☐	☐	☐
☐	☐	☐
☐	☐	☐

DATE _____

THURSDAY	FRIDAY	SATURDAY / SUNDAY
☐	☐	☐
☐	☐	☐
☐	☐	☐
☐	☐	☐
☐	☐	☐

DATE _____

Newsletter Thoughts

DATE _____

Book Promotion Plans

DATE _____

WRITING GOALS

....
....
....
....
....
....
....
....
....

SOCIAL MEDIA GOALS

f
....
....
....
....

t
....
....
....
....

Ig
....
....
....
....

BLOGGING GOALS

....
....
....
....
....
....
....

P
....
....
....
....

> "Where the Internet is about availability of information, blogging is about making information creation available to anyone."
>
> ~George Siemens

IMPORTANT ACTIVITIES FOR TODAY

☐ ....
☐ ....
☐ ....
☐ ....
☐ ....
☐ ....
☐ ....
☐ ....

DATE _____

SOCIAL MEDIA GOALS

f
....
....
....
....

t
....
....
....
....

○
....
....
....
....

p
....
....
....
....

WRITING GOALS

....
....
....
....
....
....
....
....
....
....

BLOGGING GOALS

....
....
....
....
....
....
....
....

IMPORTANT ACTIVITIES FOR TODAY

- [ ] ....
- [ ] ....
- [ ] ....
- [ ] ....
- [ ] ....
- [ ] ....
- [ ] ....
- [ ] ....

> "There are tons of different factors that go into ranking well, but the biggest is high-quality content."
>
> ~David Sinick

DATE _____

WRITING GOALS

BLOGGING GOALS

SOCIAL MEDIA GOALS

Facebook

Twitter

Instagram

Pinterest

IMPORTANT ACTIVITIES FOR TODAY

- [ ]
- [ ]
- [ ]
- [ ]
- [ ]
- [ ]
- [ ]
- [ ]

> "Your ultimate consumers are your users, not search engines."
>
> ~Google's SEO Starter Guide

DATE _____

SOCIAL MEDIA GOALS

f
....
....
....
....

🐦
....
....
....
....

📷
....
....
....
....

P
....
....
....
....

WRITING GOALS

....
....
....
....
....
....
....
....
....
....

BLOGGING GOALS

....
....
....
....
....
....
....
....

IMPORTANT ACTIVITIES FOR TODAY

- [ ] ....
- [ ] ....
- [ ] ....
- [ ] ....
- [ ] ....
- [ ] ....
- [ ] ....
- [ ] ....

> "Blogging is hard because of the grind required to stay interesting and relevant."
>
> ~Sufia Tippu

DATE _____

WRITING GOALS

....
....
....
....
....
....
....
....
....
....
....
....

SOCIAL MEDIA GOALS

f
....
....
....
....

t
....
....
....
....

IG
....
....
....
....

P
....
....
....
....

BLOGGING GOALS

....
....
....
....
....
....
....

> "If you want to continually grow your blog, you need to learn to blog on a consistent basis."
>
> ~Neil Patel

IMPORTANT ACTIVITIES FOR TODAY

- [ ] ....
- [ ] ....
- [ ] ....
- [ ] ....
- [ ] ....
- [ ] ....
- [ ] ....
- [ ] ....

DATE _____

SOCIAL MEDIA GOALS

f
....
....
....
....

t
....
....
....
....

ig
....
....
....
....

p
....
....
....
....

WRITING GOALS

....
....
....
....
....
....
....
....
....
....
....
....

BLOGGING GOALS

....
....
....
....
....
....
....

IMPORTANT ACTIVITIES FOR TODAY

- [ ] ....
- [ ] ....
- [ ] ....
- [ ] ....
- [ ] ....
- [ ] ....
- [ ] ....
- [ ] ....

> "You can work quite hard, in particular online, and do quite well independently, but if you really want to grow you need points of leverage and most of them come from knowing people."
>
> ~Yaro Starak

DATE _____

WRITING GOALS

SOCIAL MEDIA GOALS

[Facebook]

[Twitter]

[Instagram]

[Pinterest]

BLOGGING GOALS

> "If you love writing or making music or blogging or any sort of performing art, then do it. Do it with everything you've got. Just don't plan on using it as a shortcut to making a living."
>
> ~Seth Godin

IMPORTANT ACTIVITIES FOR TODAY

- [ ]
- [ ]
- [ ]
- [ ]
- [ ]
- [ ]
- [ ]
- [ ]

DATE _____

SOCIAL MEDIA GOALS

WRITING GOALS

BLOGGING GOALS

IMPORTANT ACTIVITIES FOR TODAY

- [ ]
- [ ]
- [ ]
- [ ]
- [ ]
- [ ]
- [ ]
- [ ]

"Social media is not a fad because it's human."

~ Gary Vaynerchuk

DATE _____

WRITING GOALS

BLOGGING GOALS

SOCIAL MEDIA GOALS

IMPORTANT ACTIVITIES FOR TODAY

- [ ]
- [ ]
- [ ]
- [ ]
- [ ]
- [ ]
- [ ]
- [ ]

> "Successful blogging is not about one time hits. It's about building a loyal following over time."
>
> ~David Aston

DATE _____

SOCIAL MEDIA GOALS

f
....
....
....
....

🐦
....
....
....
....

📷
....
....
....
....

P
....
....
....
....

WRITING GOALS
....
....
....
....
....
....
....
....
....
....

BLOGGING GOALS
....
....
....
....
....
....
....
....

IMPORTANT ACTIVITIES FOR TODAY

- [ ] ....
- [ ] ....
- [ ] ....
- [ ] ....
- [ ] ....
- [ ] ....
- [ ] ....
- [ ] ....

> "There's a lot of information out there for free, so you've got to figure out what makes your information different."
>
> ~Matt Wolfe

DATE _____

WRITING GOALS

SOCIAL MEDIA GOALS

BLOGGING GOALS

IMPORTANT ACTIVITIES FOR TODAY

- [ ]
- [ ]
- [ ]
- [ ]
- [ ]
- [ ]
- [ ]
- [ ]

"What you do after you create your content is what truly counts."

~Gary Vaynerchuk

DATE _____

SOCIAL MEDIA GOALS

f
....
....
....
....

t
....
....
....
....

IG
....
....
....
....

P
....
....
....
....

WRITING GOALS
....
....
....
....
....
....
....
....
....
....
....

BLOGGING GOALS
....
....
....
....
....
....
....

IMPORTANT ACTIVITIES FOR TODAY

- [ ] ....
- [ ] ....
- [ ] ....
- [ ] ....
- [ ] ....
- [ ] ....
- [ ] ....
- [ ] ....

> "I've long advised that bloggers seeking to make money from blogging spread their interests across multiple revenue streams so as not to put all their eggs in one basket."
>
> ~Darren Rowse

DATE _____

WRITING GOALS

SOCIAL MEDIA GOALS

BLOGGING GOALS

IMPORTANT ACTIVITIES FOR TODAY

- [ ]
- [ ]
- [ ]
- [ ]
- [ ]
- [ ]
- [ ]
- [ ]
- [ ]

> "The currency of blogging is authenticity and trust."
>
> ~Jason Calacanis

DATE _____

SOCIAL MEDIA GOALS

WRITING GOALS

BLOGGING GOALS

IMPORTANT ACTIVITIES FOR TODAY

- [ ]
- [ ]
- [ ]
- [ ]
- [ ]
- [ ]
- [ ]
- [ ]

"Blogging is not a business by itself, it is only a promotional platform."

~David Risley

DATE _____

WRITING GOALS

....
....
....
....
....
....
....
....
....
....
....

BLOGGING GOALS

....
....
....
....
....
....
....

SOCIAL MEDIA GOALS

f
....
....
....

t
....
....
....

ig
....
....
....

p
....
....

> "Successful people don't spam."
> ~Adrienne Smith

IMPORTANT ACTIVITIES FOR TODAY

- [ ] ....
- [ ] ....
- [ ] ....
- [ ] ....
- [ ] ....
- [ ] ....
- [ ] ....
- [ ] ....

DATE _____

SOCIAL MEDIA GOALS

f

t

Ig

P

WRITING GOALS

BLOGGING GOALS

IMPORTANT ACTIVITIES FOR TODAY

- [ ]
- [ ]
- [ ]
- [ ]
- [ ]
- [ ]
- [ ]
- [ ]

> "Blogging is good for your career. A well-executed blog sets you apart as an expert in your field."
>
> ~Penelope Trunk

DATE _____

WRITING GOALS

SOCIAL MEDIA GOALS

BLOGGING GOALS

IMPORTANT ACTIVITIES FOR TODAY

- [ ]
- [ ]
- [ ]
- [ ]
- [ ]
- [ ]
- [ ]
- [ ]

> "A well-maintained blog establishes your authority in a niche by showcasing your knowledge and dedication to the topic."
>
> ~Penelope Trunk

DATE _____

SOCIAL MEDIA GOALS

f
....
....
....
....

🐦
....
....
....
....

📷
....
....
....
....

P
....
....
....
....

WRITING GOALS

....
....
....
....
....
....
....
....
....

BLOGGING GOALS

....
....
....
....
....
....
....

IMPORTANT ACTIVITIES FOR TODAY

- [ ] ....
- [ ] ....
- [ ] ....
- [ ] ....
- [ ] ....
- [ ] ....
- [ ] ....
- [ ] ....

> "The internet has no eraser."
>
> ~Liz Strauss

DATE _____

WRITING GOALS

BLOGGING GOALS

SOCIAL MEDIA GOALS

[Facebook]

[Twitter]

[Instagram]

[Pinterest]

> "In truth, the real opportunities for building authority and buzz thorugh social meida have only just begun. You simply have to look and see where things are going instead of where they've been."
>
> ~Brian Clark

IMPORTANT ACTIVITIES FOR TODAY

- [ ]
- [ ]
- [ ]
- [ ]
- [ ]
- [ ]
- [ ]
- [ ]

DATE _____

SOCIAL MEDIA GOALS

WRITING GOALS

BLOGGING GOALS

IMPORTANT ACTIVITIES FOR TODAY

- [ ]
- [ ]
- [ ]
- [ ]
- [ ]
- [ ]
- [ ]
- [ ]

> "Selling to people through social media is like going to a party, meeting somebody for the first time, and then saying, "Hey, do you want to buy this Tupperware?"
>
> ~Pat Flynn

DATE _____

WRITING GOALS

BLOGGING GOALS

SOCIAL MEDIA GOALS

Facebook

Twitter

Instagram

Pinterest

"Visual content is 40 times more likely to be shared on social media than any other type of content."

IMPORTANT ACTIVITIES FOR TODAY

- [ ]
- [ ]
- [ ]
- [ ]
- [ ]
- [ ]
- [ ]
- [ ]
- [ ]

DATE _____

SOCIAL MEDIA GOALS

f

🐦

📷

P

WRITING GOALS

BLOGGING GOALS

IMPORTANT ACTIVITIES FOR TODAY

- [ ]
- [ ]
- [ ]
- [ ]
- [ ]
- [ ]
- [ ]
- [ ]

> "Social media is not a media. The key is to listen, engage, and build relationships."
>
> ~David Alston

DATE _____

WRITING GOALS

SOCIAL MEDIA GOALS

BLOGGING GOALS

IMPORTANT ACTIVITIES FOR TODAY

- [ ]
- [ ]
- [ ]
- [ ]
- [ ]
- [ ]
- [ ]
- [ ]

> "Engage rather than sell ... Work as a co-creator, not a marketer."
>
> ~Tom H.C. Anderson

DATE _____

SOCIAL MEDIA GOALS

WRITING GOALS

BLOGGING GOALS

IMPORTANT ACTIVITIES FOR TODAY

- [ ]
- [ ]
- [ ]
- [ ]
- [ ]
- [ ]
- [ ]
- [ ]

> "Activate your fans, don't just collect them like baseball cards."
>
> ~Jay Baer

DATE _____

WRITING GOALS

BLOGGING GOALS

SOCIAL MEDIA GOALS

IMPORTANT ACTIVITIES FOR TODAY

- [ ]
- [ ]
- [ ]
- [ ]
- [ ]
- [ ]
- [ ]
- [ ]

"Focus on how to be social, not on how to do social."

~Jay Baer

DATE _____

SOCIAL MEDIA GOALS

f

t

◙

P

WRITING GOALS

BLOGGING GOALS

IMPORTANT ACTIVITIES FOR TODAY

- [ ]
- [ ]
- [ ]
- [ ]
- [ ]
- [ ]
- [ ]
- [ ]

> "If you make customers unhappy in the physical world, they might each tell 6 friends. If you make customers unhappy on the Internet, they can each tell 6,000 friends."
>
> ~Jeff Bezos

DATE _____

WRITING GOALS

SOCIAL MEDIA GOALS

[Facebook]

[Twitter]

[Instagram]

[Pinterest]

BLOGGING GOALS

"Don't say anything on-line that you wouldn't want plastered on a billboard with your face on it."

~Erin Bury

IMPORTANT ACTIVITIES FOR TODAY

- [ ]
- [ ]
- [ ]
- [ ]
- [ ]
- [ ]
- [ ]
- [ ]

DATE _____

SOCIAL MEDIA GOALS

Facebook

....
....
....
....

Twitter

....
....
....
....

Instagram

....
....
....
....

Pinterest

....
....
....
....

WRITING GOALS

....
....
....
....
....
....
....
....
....
....
....

BLOGGING GOALS

....
....
....
....
....
....
....
....

IMPORTANT ACTIVITIES FOR TODAY

- [ ] ....
- [ ] ....
- [ ] ....
- [ ] ....
- [ ] ....
- [ ] ....
- [ ] ....
- [ ] ....

> "'Build it, and they will come' only works in the movies. Social Media is a 'build it, nurture it, engage them, and they may come and stay.'"
>
> ~Seth Godin

DATE _____

WRITING GOALS

SOCIAL MEDIA GOALS

BLOGGING GOALS

> "Conversations among the members of your marketplace happen whether you like it or not. Good marketing encourages the right sort of conversations.'"
>
> ~Seth Godin

IMPORTANT ACTIVITIES FOR TODAY

- [ ]
- [ ]
- [ ]
- [ ]
- [ ]
- [ ]
- [ ]
- [ ]

DATE _____

SOCIAL MEDIA GOALS

[Facebook]

[Twitter]

[Instagram]

[Pinterest]

WRITING GOALS

BLOGGING GOALS

IMPORTANT ACTIVITIES FOR TODAY

- [ ]
- [ ]
- [ ]
- [ ]
- [ ]
- [ ]
- [ ]
- [ ]

> "Social Media is about the people! Not about your business. Provide for the people and the people will provide for you."
>
> ~Matt Goulart

DATE _____

MONDAY	TUESDAY	WEDNESDAY
☐	☐	☐
☐	☐	☐
☐	☐	☐
☐	☐	☐
☐	☐	☐

DATE _____

THURSDAY	FRIDAY	SATURDAY / SUNDAY
☐	☐	☐
☐	☐	☐
☐	☐	☐
☐	☐	☐
☐	☐	☐

DATE _____

Newsletter Thoughts

DATE _____

Book Promotion Plans

DATE _____

WRITING GOALS

SOCIAL MEDIA GOALS

BLOGGING GOALS

IMPORTANT ACTIVITIES FOR TODAY

- [ ]
- [ ]
- [ ]
- [ ]
- [ ]
- [ ]
- [ ]
- [ ]

> "The value of being connected and transparent is so high that the roadbumps of privacy issues are much lower in actual experience than people's fears."
>
> ~Reid Hoffman

DATE _____

SOCIAL MEDIA GOALS

Facebook

....
....
....
....

Twitter

....
....
....
....

Instagram

....
....
....
....

Pinterest

....
....
....
....

WRITING GOALS

....
....
....
....
....
....
....
....
....
....

BLOGGING GOALS

....
....
....
....
....
....
....

IMPORTANT ACTIVITIES FOR TODAY

- [ ] ....
- [ ] ....
- [ ] ....
- [ ] ....
- [ ] ....
- [ ] ....
- [ ] ....
- [ ] ....

> "Bring the best of your authentic self to every opportunity."
>
> ~Brian Jantsch

DATE _____

WRITING GOALS

SOCIAL MEDIA GOALS

BLOGGING GOALS

IMPORTANT ACTIVITIES FOR TODAY

- [ ]
- [ ]
- [ ]
- [ ]
- [ ]
- [ ]
- [ ]
- [ ]

> "Just be nice, take genuine interest in the people you meet, and keep in touch with people you like. This will create a group of people who are invested in helping you because they know you and appreciate you."
>
> ~Guy Kawasaki

DATE _____

SOCIAL MEDIA GOALS

WRITING GOALS

BLOGGING GOALS

IMPORTANT ACTIVITIES FOR TODAY

- [ ]
- [ ]
- [ ]
- [ ]
- [ ]
- [ ]
- [ ]
- [ ]

> "What happens in Vegas stays in Vegas; what happens on Twitter stays on Google forever!"
>
> ~Jure Klepic

DATE _____

WRITING GOALS

....
....
....
....
....
....
....
....
....
....

BLOGGING GOALS

....
....
....
....
....
....
....
....

SOCIAL MEDIA GOALS

f
....
....
....
....

Twitter
....
....
....

Instagram
....
....
....

Pinterest
....
....
....

> "Most bloggers who rise above the clutter are quite often prolific – they work hard, not just writing content but networking, engaging in Social Media and more."
>
> ~ Darren Rowse

IMPORTANT ACTIVITIES FOR TODAY

☐ ....
☐ ....
☐ ....
☐ ....
☐ ....
☐ ....
☐ ....
☐ ....

DATE _____

SOCIAL MEDIA GOALS

f
....
....
....
....

t
....
....
....
....

ig
....
....
....
....

p
....
....
....
....

WRITING GOALS

....
....
....
....
....
....
....
....
....
....
....
....

BLOGGING GOALS

....
....
....
....
....
....
....
....

IMPORTANT ACTIVITIES FOR TODAY

☐ ....
☐ ....
☐ ....
☐ ....
☐ ....
☐ ....
☐ ....
☐ ....

> "There are no magic wands, no hidden tracks, and no secret handshakes that can bring you immediate success, but with time, energy and determination you can get there."
>
> ~Darren Rowse

DATE _____

WRITING GOALS

....
....
....
....
....
....
....
....
....

BLOGGING GOALS

....
....
....
....
....
....

SOCIAL MEDIA GOALS

f
....
....
....

t
....
....
....

ig
....
....
....

p
....
....
....

> "The qualities that make Twitter seem insane and half-baked are what makes it so powerful."
> ~Jonathan Zittrain

IMPORTANT ACTIVITIES FOR TODAY

- [ ] ....
- [ ] ....
- [ ] ....
- [ ] ....
- [ ] ....
- [ ] ....
- [ ] ....
- [ ] ....

DATE _____

SOCIAL MEDIA GOALS

f
....
....
....
....

t
....
....
....
....

ig
....
....
....
....

p
....
....
....
....

WRITING GOALS

....
....
....
....
....
....
....
....
....
....
....

BLOGGING GOALS

....
....
....
....
....
....
....
....

IMPORTANT ACTIVITIES FOR TODAY

- [ ] ....
- [ ] ....
- [ ] ....
- [ ] ....
- [ ] ....
- [ ] ....
- [ ] ....
- [ ] ....

> "When you give everyone a voice and give people power, the system usually ends up in a really good place."
>
> ~Mark Zuckerberg

DATE _____

WRITING GOALS

....
....
....
....
....
....
....
....
....
....

BLOGGING GOALS

....
....
....
....
....
....
....

SOCIAL MEDIA GOALS

f
....
....
....
....

Twitter
....
....
....
....

Instagram
....
....
....
....

Pinterest
....
....
....
....

"Never underestimate the vital importance of finding early in life the work that for you is play. This turns possible underachievers into happy warriors."

~ Jeff Bullas

IMPORTANT ACTIVITIES FOR TODAY

- [ ] ....
- [ ] ....
- [ ] ....
- [ ] ....
- [ ] ....
- [ ] ....
- [ ] ....
- [ ] ....

DATE _____

SOCIAL MEDIA GOALS

WRITING GOALS

BLOGGING GOALS

IMPORTANT ACTIVITIES FOR TODAY

- [ ]
- [ ]
- [ ]
- [ ]
- [ ]
- [ ]
- [ ]
- [ ]

> "Social media is here. It's not going away; not a passing fad. Be where your customers are: in social media."
>
> ~Lori Ruff

DATE _____

WRITING GOALS

SOCIAL MEDIA GOALS

BLOGGING GOALS

IMPORTANT ACTIVITIES FOR TODAY

- [ ]
- [ ]
- [ ]
- [ ]
- [ ]
- [ ]
- [ ]
- [ ]

> "Most of us have experienced wow moments. We just haven't taken time to think deeply about them."
>
> ~Michael Hyatt

DATE _____

SOCIAL MEDIA GOALS

f

t

○

P

WRITING GOALS

BLOGGING GOALS

IMPORTANT ACTIVITIES FOR TODAY

- [ ]
- [ ]
- [ ]
- [ ]
- [ ]
- [ ]
- [ ]
- [ ]
- [ ]

> "On engagement, we're already seeing that mobile users are more likely to be daily active users than desktop users. They're more likely to use Facebook six or seven days of the week."
>
> ~Mark Zuckerberg

DATE _____

WRITING GOALS

....
....
....
....
....
....
....
....
....
....
....
....

BLOGGING GOALS

....
....
....
....
....
....
....

SOCIAL MEDIA GOALS

f
....
....
....
....

twitter
....
....
....
....

instagram
....
....
....
....

pinterest
....
....
....
....

> "Facebook is not your friend. It is a surveillance engine."
> ~Richard Stallman

IMPORTANT ACTIVITIES FOR TODAY

- [ ] ....
- [ ] ....
- [ ] ....
- [ ] ....
- [ ] ....
- [ ] ....
- [ ] ....
- [ ] ....

DATE _____

SOCIAL MEDIA GOALS

f
....
....
....
....

t
....
....
....
....

ig
....
....
....
....

p
....
....
....
....

WRITING GOALS

....
....
....
....
....
....
....
....
....
....

BLOGGING GOALS

....
....
....
....
....
....
....

IMPORTANT ACTIVITIES FOR TODAY

- [ ] ....
- [ ] ....
- [ ] ....
- [ ] ....
- [ ] ....
- [ ] ....
- [ ] ....
- [ ] ....

> "Twitter is not a technology, it's a conversation – and it's happening with or without you."
>
> ~Charlene Li, author

DATE _____

WRITING GOALS

BLOGGING GOALS

SOCIAL MEDIA GOALS

IMPORTANT ACTIVITIES FOR TODAY

- [ ]
- [ ]
- [ ]
- [ ]
- [ ]
- [ ]
- [ ]
- [ ]

"When you've got 5 minutes to fill, Twitter is a great way to fill 35 minutes."

~Matt Cutts

DATE _____

SOCIAL MEDIA GOALS

f

t

IG

P

WRITING GOALS

BLOGGING GOALS

IMPORTANT ACTIVITIES FOR TODAY

- [ ]
- [ ]
- [ ]
- [ ]
- [ ]
- [ ]
- [ ]
- [ ]

> "Social media is not just a spoke on the wheel of marketing. It's becoming the way entire bicycles are built."
>
> ~Ryan Lilly, author

DATE _____

WRITING GOALS

BLOGGING GOALS

SOCIAL MEDIA GOALS

IMPORTANT ACTIVITIES FOR TODAY

- [ ]
- [ ]
- [ ]
- [ ]
- [ ]
- [ ]
- [ ]
- [ ]

> "Social media will help you build up the loyalty of your current customers to the point that they will willingly, and for free, tell others about you."
>
> ~Bonnie Sainsbury

DATE _____

SOCIAL MEDIA GOALS

WRITING GOALS

BLOGGING GOALS

IMPORTANT ACTIVITIES FOR TODAY

- [ ]
- [ ]
- [ ]
- [ ]
- [ ]
- [ ]
- [ ]
- [ ]

> "The Art of Twitter is in the Re-tweet. You Must be Interesting."
>
> ~Peter Shankman

DATE _____

WRITING GOALS

SOCIAL MEDIA GOALS

[Facebook]

[Twitter]

[Instagram]

BLOGGING GOALS

[Pinterest]

"It's important to think of every customer as an on-line celebrity with followers, friends, & above all, influence."

~Dave Kerpen

IMPORTANT ACTIVITIES FOR TODAY

☐
☐
☐
☐
☐
☐
☐
☐

DATE _____

SOCIAL MEDIA GOALS

f
....
....
....
....

🐦
....
....
....
....

📷
....
....
....
....

P
....
....
....
....

WRITING GOALS

....
....
....
....
....
....
....
....
....
....

BLOGGING GOALS

....
....
....
....
....
....
....

IMPORTANT ACTIVITIES FOR TODAY

- [ ] ....
- [ ] ....
- [ ] ....
- [ ] ....
- [ ] ....
- [ ] ....
- [ ] ....
- [ ] ....

> "As with any relationship, the market favors those who give more value than they ask for."
>
> ~Leslie Bradshaw

DATE _____

WRITING GOALS

SOCIAL MEDIA GOALS

BLOGGING GOALS

IMPORTANT ACTIVITIES FOR TODAY

- [ ]
- [ ]
- [ ]
- [ ]
- [ ]
- [ ]
- [ ]
- [ ]

"The ultimate content strategy is listening."

– Marcus Sheridan

DATE _____

SOCIAL MEDIA GOALS

WRITING GOALS

BLOGGING GOALS

IMPORTANT ACTIVITIES FOR TODAY

- [ ]
- [ ]
- [ ]
- [ ]
- [ ]
- [ ]
- [ ]
- [ ]

> "You're never as smart as you think you are when you are winning and never as dumb as you feel when you are losing."
>
> ~Michael Hyatt

DATE _____

WRITING GOALS

....
....
....
....
....
....
....
....
....

BLOGGING GOALS

....
....
....
....
....
....

SOCIAL MEDIA GOALS

f
....
....
....
....

t
....
....
....
....

IG
....
....
....
....

P
....
....
....
....

"You can't take care of anyone else unless you first take care of yourself."
~Michael Hyatt

IMPORTANT ACTIVITIES FOR TODAY

- [ ] ....
- [ ] ....
- [ ] ....
- [ ] ....
- [ ] ....
- [ ] ....
- [ ] ....
- [ ] ....

DATE _____

SOCIAL MEDIA GOALS

f

t

[ig]

P

WRITING GOALS

BLOGGING GOALS

IMPORTANT ACTIVITIES FOR TODAY

- [ ]
- [ ]
- [ ]
- [ ]
- [ ]
- [ ]
- [ ]
- [ ]

> "Courage is the willingness to act in spite of fear."
>
> ~Michael Hyatt

DATE _____

WRITING GOALS

SOCIAL MEDIA GOALS

BLOGGING GOALS

IMPORTANT ACTIVITIES FOR TODAY

- [ ]
- [ ]
- [ ]
- [ ]
- [ ]
- [ ]
- [ ]
- [ ]

"Make sure your worst enemy doesn't live between your two ears."

~Laird Hamilton

DATE _____

SOCIAL MEDIA GOALS

WRITING GOALS

BLOGGING GOALS

IMPORTANT ACTIVITIES FOR TODAY

- [ ]
- [ ]
- [ ]
- [ ]
- [ ]
- [ ]
- [ ]
- [ ]

"The greatest danger for most of us is not that we aim too high and we miss it, but we aim too low and reach it."

~Michelangelo

DATE _____

WRITING GOALS

....
....
....
....
....
....
....
....
....
....

BLOGGING GOALS

....
....
....
....
....
....
....

SOCIAL MEDIA GOALS

f
....
....
....
....

t
....
....
....
....

IG
....
....
....

P
....
....

> "You don't need more opportunity. You need to learn to execute on the opportunities you already have."
>
> ~Michael Hyatt

IMPORTANT ACTIVITIES FOR TODAY

☐ ....
☐ ....
☐ ....
☐ ....
☐ ....
☐ ....
☐ ....
☐ ....

DATE _____

SOCIAL MEDIA GOALS

f
....
....
....
....

🐦
....
....
....
....

📷
....
....
....
....

P
....
....
....
....

WRITING GOALS

....
....
....
....
....
....
....
....
....
....

BLOGGING GOALS

....
....
....
....
....
....
....
....

IMPORTANT ACTIVITIES FOR TODAY

- [ ] ....
- [ ] ....
- [ ] ....
- [ ] ....
- [ ] ....
- [ ] ....
- [ ] ....
- [ ] ....

> "You can't start the next chapter of your life if you keep re-reading the last one."
>
> ~Anonymous

DATE _____

WRITING GOALS

BLOGGING GOALS

SOCIAL MEDIA GOALS

IMPORTANT ACTIVITIES FOR TODAY

- [ ]
- [ ]
- [ ]
- [ ]
- [ ]
- [ ]
- [ ]
- [ ]

> "In a crowded marketplace, fitting in a failure. In a busy marketplace, not standing out is the same as being invisible."
>
> ~Seth Godin

DATE _____

SOCIAL MEDIA GOALS

f

t

Ig

P

WRITING GOALS

BLOGGING GOALS

IMPORTANT ACTIVITIES FOR TODAY

- [ ]
- [ ]
- [ ]
- [ ]
- [ ]
- [ ]
- [ ]
- [ ]

> "I learned that a long walk and calm conversation are an incredible combination if you want to build a bridge."
>
> ~Seth Godin

DATE _____

MONDAY	TUESDAY	WEDNESDAY
☐	☐	☐
☐	☐	☐
☐	☐	☐
☐	☐	☐
☐	☐	☐

DATE _____

THURSDAY	FRIDAY	SATURDAY / SUNDAY
☐	☐	☐
☐	☐	☐
☐	☐	☐
☐	☐	☐
☐	☐	☐

DATE _____

Newsletter Thoughts

DATE _____

Book Promotion Plans

DATE _____

WRITING GOALS

....
....
....
....
....
....
....
....
....
....
....

BLOGGING GOALS

....
....
....
....
....
....
....

SOCIAL MEDIA GOALS

f
....
....
....
....

t
....
....
....
....

IG
....
....
....
....

p
....
....
....
....

> "Marketing is a contest for people's attention."
> ~Seth Godin

IMPORTANT ACTIVITIES FOR TODAY

☐ ....
☐ ....
☐ ....
☐ ....
☐ ....
☐ ....
☐ ....
☐ ....

DATE _____

SOCIAL MEDIA GOALS

[Facebook]

[Twitter]

[Instagram]

[Pinterest]

WRITING GOALS

BLOGGING GOALS

IMPORTANT ACTIVITIES FOR TODAY

- [ ]
- [ ]
- [ ]
- [ ]
- [ ]
- [ ]
- [ ]
- [ ]

> "I think the most productive thing to do during times of change is to be your best self, not the best version of someone else."
>
> ~Seth Godin

DATE _____

WRITING GOALS

SOCIAL MEDIA GOALS

BLOGGING GOALS

IMPORTANT ACTIVITIES FOR TODAY

- [ ]
- [ ]
- [ ]
- [ ]
- [ ]
- [ ]
- [ ]
- [ ]

> "Do you know what people want more than anything? They want to be missed. They want to be missed the day they don't show up. They want to be missed when they're gone."
>
> ~Seth Godin

DATE _____

SOCIAL MEDIA GOALS

f
....
....
....
....

t
....
....
....
....

i
....
....
....
....

p
....
....
....
....

WRITING GOALS

....
....
....
....
....
....
....
....
....
....

BLOGGING GOALS

....
....
....
....
....
....
....

IMPORTANT ACTIVITIES FOR TODAY

- [ ] ....
- [ ] ....
- [ ] ....
- [ ] ....
- [ ] ....
- [ ] ....
- [ ] ....
- [ ] ....

> "One reason I encourage people to blog is that the act of doing it stretches your available vocabulary and hones a new voice."
>
> ~Seth Godin

DATE _____

WRITING GOALS

SOCIAL MEDIA GOALS

BLOGGING GOALS

IMPORTANT ACTIVITIES FOR TODAY

- [ ]
- [ ]
- [ ]
- [ ]
- [ ]
- [ ]
- [ ]
- [ ]

> "Permission marketing turns strangers into friends and friends into loyal customers. It's not just about entertainment – it's about education. Permission marketing is curriculum marketing."
>
> ~Seth Godin

DATE _____

SOCIAL MEDIA GOALS

f
....
....
....
....

t
....
....
....
....

ig
....
....
....
....

p
....
....
....
....

WRITING GOALS

....
....
....
....
....
....
....
....
....
....
....

BLOGGING GOALS

....
....
....
....
....
....
....

IMPORTANT ACTIVITIES FOR TODAY

- [ ] ....
- [ ] ....
- [ ] ....
- [ ] ....
- [ ] ....
- [ ] ....
- [ ] ....
- [ ] ....

> "I made a decision to write for my readers, not to try to find more readers for my writing."
>
> ~Seth Godin

DATE _____

WRITING GOALS

SOCIAL MEDIA GOALS

BLOGGING GOALS

"Stop getting distracted by things that have nothing to do with your dreams."

IMPORTANT ACTIVITIES FOR TODAY

- [ ]
- [ ]
- [ ]
- [ ]
- [ ]
- [ ]
- [ ]
- [ ]

DATE _____

SOCIAL MEDIA GOALS

f
....
....
....
....

t
....
....
....
....

ig
....
....
....
....

p
....
....
....

WRITING GOALS

....
....
....
....
....
....
....
....
....
....

BLOGGING GOALS

....
....
....
....
....
....
....

IMPORTANT ACTIVITIES FOR TODAY

- [ ] ....
- [ ] ....
- [ ] ....
- [ ] ....
- [ ] ....
- [ ] ....
- [ ] ....
- [ ] ....

> "Stop telling yourself you don't know what to do. Yes, you do. Listen to your intuition and trust yourself."
>
> ~Katherine Sullivan

DATE _____

WRITING GOALS

BLOGGING GOALS

SOCIAL MEDIA GOALS

[Facebook]

[Twitter]

[Instagram]

[Pinterest]

IMPORTANT ACTIVITIES FOR TODAY

- [ ]
- [ ]
- [ ]
- [ ]
- [ ]
- [ ]
- [ ]
- [ ]

> "Don't ask people for directions when they've never been where you are going."
>
> ~Katherine Sullivan

DATE _____

SOCIAL MEDIA GOALS

WRITING GOALS

BLOGGING GOALS

IMPORTANT ACTIVITIES FOR TODAY

- [ ]
- [ ]
- [ ]
- [ ]
- [ ]
- [ ]
- [ ]
- [ ]

> "Don't use social media to impress people; use it to impact people."
>
> ~Dave Willis

DATE _____

WRITING GOALS

....
....
....
....
....
....
....
....
....
....

BLOGGING GOALS

....
....
....
....
....
....

SOCIAL MEDIA GOALS

....
....
....

....
....
....

....
....
....

....
....
....

"Be Authentic."

IMPORTANT ACTIVITIES FOR TODAY

☐ ....
☐ ....
☐ ....
☐ ....
☐ ....
☐ ....
☐ ....
☐ ....

DATE _____

SOCIAL MEDIA GOALS

f

t

📷

P

WRITING GOALS

BLOGGING GOALS

IMPORTANT ACTIVITIES FOR TODAY

☐
☐
☐
☐
☐
☐
☐
☐

> "A goal should scare you a little, & excite you A LOT."
>
> ~Joe Vitale

DATE _____

WRITING GOALS

....
....
....
....
....
....
....
....
....
....

BLOGGING GOALS

....
....
....
....
....
....
....

SOCIAL MEDIA GOALS

f
....
....
....
....

t
....
....
....
....

ig
....
....
....
....

p
....
....
....
....

"Surround yourself with those on the same mission as you."

IMPORTANT ACTIVITIES FOR TODAY

☐ ....
☐ ....
☐ ....
☐ ....
☐ ....
☐ ....
☐ ....
☐ ....

DATE _____

SOCIAL MEDIA GOALS

f

t

◻

P

WRITING GOALS

BLOGGING GOALS

IMPORTANT ACTIVITIES FOR TODAY

- ☐
- ☐
- ☐
- ☐
- ☐
- ☐
- ☐
- ☐

> "It's your road, and yours alone. Others may walk it with you, but no one can walk it for you."
>
> ~Rumi

DATE _____

WRITING GOALS

....
....
....
....
....
....
....
....
....
....
....
....

BLOGGING GOALS

....
....
....
....
....
....

SOCIAL MEDIA GOALS

f
....
....
....

t
....
....
....

Ig
....
....
....

P
....
....
....

> "Never think that what you have to offer is insignificant. There will always be someone out there that needs what you have to give."

IMPORTANT ACTIVITIES FOR TODAY

- [ ] ....
- [ ] ....
- [ ] ....
- [ ] ....
- [ ] ....
- [ ] ....
- [ ] ....
- [ ] ....

DATE _____

SOCIAL MEDIA GOALS

f
....
....
....
....

t
....
....
....
....

ig
....
....
....
....

p
....
....
....
....

WRITING GOALS

....
....
....
....
....
....
....
....
....

BLOGGING GOALS

....
....
....
....
....
....
....

IMPORTANT ACTIVITIES FOR TODAY

- [ ] ....
- [ ] ....
- [ ] ....
- [ ] ....
- [ ] ....
- [ ] ....
- [ ] ....
- [ ] ....

> "Without strategy, content is just stuff, and the world has enough stuff."
>
> ~ @arjunbasu

DATE _____

WRITING GOALS

BLOGGING GOALS

SOCIAL MEDIA GOALS

f

t

Instagram

P

> "Marketing is enthusiasm transferred to the customer."
> ~Gregory Ciotti

IMPORTANT ACTIVITIES FOR TODAY

- [ ]
- [ ]
- [ ]
- [ ]
- [ ]
- [ ]
- [ ]
- [ ]

DATE _____

SOCIAL MEDIA GOALS

f
....
....
....
....

t
....
....
....
....

IG
....
....
....
....

P
....
....
....
....

WRITING GOALS

....
....
....
....
....
....
....
....
....
....
....

BLOGGING GOALS

....
....
....
....
....
....
....

IMPORTANT ACTIVITIES FOR TODAY

☐ ....
☐ ....
☐ ....
☐ ....
☐ ....
☐ ....
☐ ....
☐ ....

> "People do not buy goods and services. They buy relations, stories and magic."
>
> ~Seth Godin

DATE _____

WRITING GOALS

....
....
....
....
....
....
....
....
....
....
....

BLOGGING GOALS

....
....
....
....
....
....
....

SOCIAL MEDIA GOALS

f
....
....
....

twitter
....
....
....

instagram
....
....
....

pinterest
....
....
....

"Stop selling, start helping."
~Zig Zigler

IMPORTANT ACTIVITIES FOR TODAY

☐ ....
☐ ....
☐ ....
☐ ....
☐ ....
☐ ....
☐ ....
☐ ....

DATE _____

SOCIAL MEDIA GOALS

[Facebook]

[Twitter]

[Instagram]

[Pinterest]

WRITING GOALS

BLOGGING GOALS

IMPORTANT ACTIVITIES FOR TODAY

- [ ]
- [ ]
- [ ]
- [ ]
- [ ]
- [ ]
- [ ]
- [ ]

> "Marketing is no longer about the stuff yo make, but about the stories you tell."
>
> ~Seth Godin

DATE _____

WRITING GOALS

....
....
....
....
....
....
....
....
....
....
....

BLOGGING GOALS

....
....
....
....
....
....
....
....

SOCIAL MEDIA GOALS

f
....
....
....
....

t
....
....
....
....

ig
....
....
....
....

p
....
....
....
....

"Don't deliver a Product – Deliver an Experience."

IMPORTANT ACTIVITIES FOR TODAY

☐ ....
☐ ....
☐ ....
☐ ....
☐ ....
☐ ....
☐ ....
☐ ....

DATE _____

SOCIAL MEDIA GOALS

f
....
....
....
....

t
....
....
....
....

ig
....
....
....
....

p
....
....
....
....

WRITING GOALS
....
....
....
....
....
....
....
....
....
....

BLOGGING GOALS
....
....
....
....
....
....
....

IMPORTANT ACTIVITIES FOR TODAY
- [ ] ....
- [ ] ....
- [ ] ....
- [ ] ....
- [ ] ....
- [ ] ....
- [ ] ....
- [ ] ....

> "Strive not to be a success, but rather to be of value."
>
> ~Albert Einstein

DATE _____

WRITING GOALS

SOCIAL MEDIA GOALS

BLOGGING GOALS

IMPORTANT ACTIVITIES FOR TODAY

- [ ]
- [ ]
- [ ]
- [ ]
- [ ]
- [ ]
- [ ]
- [ ]

"Be a resource, not a sales pitch."

DATE _____

SOCIAL MEDIA GOALS

f

🐦

📷

P

WRITING GOALS

BLOGGING GOALS

IMPORTANT ACTIVITIES FOR TODAY

- [ ]
- [ ]
- [ ]
- [ ]
- [ ]
- [ ]
- [ ]
- [ ]

> "The best marketing strategy ever: CARE."
> ~Gary Vaynerchuk

DATE _____

WRITING GOALS

....
....
....
....
....
....
....
....
....
....

BLOGGING GOALS

....
....
....
....
....
....
....

SOCIAL MEDIA GOALS

f
....
....
....
....

t
....
....
....
....

ig
....
....
....

p
....
....
....

"Branding is what people say about you when you are not in the room."

IMPORTANT ACTIVITIES FOR TODAY

☐ ....
☐ ....
☐ ....
☐ ....
☐ ....
☐ ....
☐ ....
☐ ....

DATE _____

SOCIAL MEDIA GOALS

[f]
....
....
....
....

[twitter]
....
....
....
....

[instagram]
....
....
....
....

[pinterest]
....
....
....
....

WRITING GOALS

....
....
....
....
....
....
....
....
....
....

BLOGGING GOALS

....
....
....
....
....
....
....

IMPORTANT ACTIVITIES FOR TODAY

- [ ] ....
- [ ] ....
- [ ] ....
- [ ] ....
- [ ] ....
- [ ] ....
- [ ] ....
- [ ] ....

> "Marketing without data is like driving with your eyes closed."
>
> ~ Dan Zarella

DATE _____

WRITING GOALS

BLOGGING GOALS

SOCIAL MEDIA GOALS

IMPORTANT ACTIVITIES FOR TODAY

- [ ]
- [ ]
- [ ]
- [ ]
- [ ]
- [ ]
- [ ]
- [ ]
- [ ]

> "Everyone is not your customer."
> ~Seth Godin

DATE _____

SOCIAL MEDIA GOALS

f
....
....
....
....

t
....
....
....
....

○
....
....
....
....

P
....
....
....
....

WRITING GOALS

....
....
....
....
....
....
....
....
....
....

BLOGGING GOALS

....
....
....
....
....
....
....
....

IMPORTANT ACTIVITIES FOR TODAY

☐ ....
☐ ....
☐ ....
☐ ....
☐ ....
☐ ....
☐ ....
☐ ....

> "To give real service, you must add something which cannot be bought or measured with money, and that is sincerity and integrity."
>
> ~Douglas Adams

DATE _____

WRITING GOALS

SOCIAL MEDIA GOALS

BLOGGING GOALS

> "Content is fire, Social Media is gasoline."
>
> ~Jay Baer

IMPORTANT ACTIVITIES FOR TODAY

- [ ]
- [ ]
- [ ]
- [ ]
- [ ]
- [ ]
- [ ]
- [ ]

DATE _____

SOCIAL MEDIA GOALS

[Facebook]

....
....
....
....

[Twitter]

....
....
....
....

[Instagram]

....
....
....
....

[Pinterest]

....
....
....
....

WRITING GOALS

....
....
....
....
....
....
....
....
....
....

BLOGGING GOALS

....
....
....
....
....
....
....

IMPORTANT ACTIVITIES FOR TODAY

- [ ] ....
- [ ] ....
- [ ] ....
- [ ] ....
- [ ] ....
- [ ] ....
- [ ] ....
- [ ] ....

> "The best advertising you can have is a loyal customer spreading the word about how incredible your business is."
>
> ~Shep Hyken

www.ingramcontent.com/pod-product-compliance
Lightning Source LLC
Chambersburg PA
CBHW081152020426
42333CB00020B/2486